America's First Big Lie

or

*Why Conservative Critics Are
Afraid of Critical Race Theory*

Larry Kenneth Alexander

Copyright © 2021 by Larry Kenneth Alexander.

All rights reserved. No part of this publication may be reproduced, distributed, or transmitted in any form or by any electronic or mechanical means, without the prior written permission of the publisher, except in the case of brief quotations embodied in critical reviews and certain other noncommercial uses permitted by copyright law.

Printed in the United States of America

ISBN: 9798538905898

Contact author at larry@idabwellscenter.net;
(651) 325-8436

Dedication

To Maynet Alexander-Brown, supporters, and activists who have fought and continue to fight.

Table of Contents

Prologue i

Britannia and the Southern Colonies Timeline ix

Chapter 1 Critical Race Theory 1

Chapter 2 Hypocritical Race Theory 27

Chapter 3 America's True Legacy 49

Chapter 4 The Constitution Reimagined 77

Chapter 5 Annualized Reckoning 109

Chapter 6 Facts are Stubborn 131

Chapter 7 Constitutional Patriotism 158

Chapter 8 Intergenerational Dodge 183

EPILOGUE 207

"What to the Slave Is the Fourth of July?" (1852) 240

BIBLIOGRAPHY 278

Prologue

Conservatives complain that when people of color or liberals talk about the role that race played in the run-up to the Declaration of Independence... they espouse an intolerance ideology called critical race theory. They then will quickly say, "so what," given the distance... America has traveled as a nation since 1776 when you offer a reasoned rejoinder. These resistive positions are anti-intellectual that muffles constructive engagement and attempts to give the founding generation an ironclad alibi for the criminal enslavement of 500,000 colonial blacks who became the bedrock of America's slave pool *after* the American Revolution and the U. S. adoption of a proslavery constitution.

Doubtlessly, the notion that critiquing America's history from the vantage point of black colonials somehow teaches intolerance and hatred of this country is a feckless and cynical deflection. Instead, critiquing America's history from the vantage point of people of color is a long-coming first step toward proving that "truth crushed to earth" shall indeed rise again. Moreover... when a nation refuses to come to terms with and honestly acknowledge the full enormity of its forebearers' actions and either believing or pretending that they can never be made accountable to those this nation harmed... this nation makes their pain, concerns and search for closure seem illegitimate and without cause or validity. Moreover, teaching critical race theory offers America an opportunity to correct its historiography.

Blanketed by a dominant cultural narrative that Revolutionary War-era blacks were slaves during colonial times based upon "colonial statutes," these 500,000 black colonials are faceless, forgotten victims of colonial tyranny... flung into a maelstrom of American history. But we, as their descendants, are potent evidence of those voices who were unjustly silenced, destroyed, and exploited. And except for our existence, their existence, contributions, suffering, and lives have been carefully airbrushed out of America's historiography.

In furtherance... the U. S. constitution is a proslavery document that protected America's slaveholding Patriots, legitimized enslaving legally free black people, and is responsible for structural racism. History supports... colonial slavery was the product of colonial government corruption, abolished by England's enactment of the *Declaratory Act of 1766* and England's Court of the King's Bench struck down colonial statutes in the case of *James Somerset v. Charles Stewart* in 1772.... and yet, children are taught the mythology of America. James Baldwin observed that "an invented past can never be used; it cracks and crumbles under the pressures of life, like clay in a season of drought."

Dubbed critical race theory... it is the Right's new Hannibal Lecter, claiming that it threatens to eat democracy. And while most Americans might see the Fourth of July as a day to celebrate... a descendant of an American slave must see this day as an annualized day of reckoning and an opportunity to bring attention to the unfulfilled idea of individual equality under the rule of law. Critical race theorists such as Frederick Douglass have long recognized that the law could be complicit in maintaining an unjust social order.

Racism is not an outdated relic of the past. Present-day critical race theorists challenge academia, thought-leaders, and government officials to acknowledge, as a first step towards ending structural racism, that the legacy of slavery, segregation, and the imposition of second-class citizenship on black Americans and other people of color continues to permeate the social fabric of this nation.

The American Bar Association (ABA) states that critical race theory (CRT) is not a noun but a verb that "critiques how the social construction of race and institutionalized racism perpetuate a racial caste system that relegates people of color to the bottom tiers."

History supports... white colonials and black colonials were equal under English law when the Declaration of Independence was adopted on July 4, 1776. Parliament's

Declaratory Act of 1766 had nullified colonial slave statutes and racialized regulations ten years earlier. The Act rendered colonial slave statutes and racialized regulations "utterly null and void to all in purposes whatsoever" and represents *true north* as it destroyed the faux legal underpinning of the white colonial supremacy government in 1766.

The slaveholding elites of the colonies whose wealth was based upon the criminal scheme of enslaving colonial-born black Englishmen and Africans and corruption of colonial government were infuriated by Parliament's *Declaratory Act of 1766* as it legislatively abolished colonial slave statutes and racialized laws. They took it out on King George III by forming an alliance with northern colonies and providing resources for a rebellion. Then, they morphed legitimate complaints of northern colonials concerning British imperial governance and blamed slavery on King George III. These disgruntled slave masters were the force that pushed for independence from England, and they sowed the seeds for revolution.

Thomas Jefferson of Virginia lamented that the British imperial government "by one Act they have suspended powers of American legislature and by another have declared they may legislate for us themselves in all cases whatsoever. These two acts alone form a basis broad enough whereon to erect a despotism of unlimited extent."

Jefferson's lamentation about the *Declaratory Act of 1766* is powerful proof of parliamentary sovereignty over colonial governmental institutions. Jefferson... the author of the Declaration of Independence, and the other founding fathers were knowledgeable that the *Declaratory Act of 1766* had nullified colonial statutes, racialized laws, and regulations and returned erstwhile black slaves to the status *quo ante.* Moreover, England's highest court had ruled slavery was not allowed and approved by the laws of this Kingdom in the *Somerset* decision and struck down colonial statutes in 1772... when they adopted the Declaration of Independence.

On July 4, 1776, when the Continental Congress adopted the historical text that

"We hold these truths to be self-evident, that all men are created equal, that their Creator endows them with unalienable Rights, that among these are Life, Liberty and the pursuit of Happiness" it did mean individual equality for black colonials since they as a people held the same legal status as white colonials under English law.

On July 8, 1776… the first public readings of the Declaration were held in Philadelphia's Independence Square to the ringing of bells and music. One year later, on July 4, 1777, Philadelphia marked "Independence Day" by adjourning Congress and celebrating with bonfires, bells, and fireworks. Further, in a June of 1826 letter sent to Roger C. Weightman, Thomas Jefferson declined an invitation to come to Washington D. C. to help celebrate the 50th anniversary of the Declaration of Independence. Jefferson, who was gravely ill and he and America's second President John Adams both died on the Fourth of July in 1826, stated this about the document:

"May it be to the world, what I believe it will be… the signal of arousing men to burst the chains… and to assume the blessings and security of self-government. That form, which we have substituted, restores the free right to the unbounded exercise of reason and freedom of opinion. All eyes are opened, or opening, to the rights of man… For ourselves, let the annual return of this day forever refresh our recollections of these rights, and an undiminished devotion to them."

In coming to terms with my colonial American roots and as James Baldwin stated "the victim who is able to articulate the situation of the victim has ceased to be a victim, he or she has become a threat"… I became purposeful as my first youthful curiosity had already piqued me to ask the question: what made my great grandfather a slave many years ago? This descendant of a colonial slave began to write.

Britannia and the Southern Colonies Timeline

10,000 years ago Cheddar Man thrived in England. He's a hunter-gatherer who had dark brown skin, blue eyes, and Negroid features.

43 AD The Roman Empire conquered England.

410 AD Roman rule ends in England.

1328 King Edward the Third marries a woman of Moorish descent... Queen Phillipa. She's England's first black Queen consort.

1215 King John signs Magna Carta. The Magna Carta prohibits slavery in England and guarantees justice for all under the rule of law throughout the British Empire.

1526 Enslaved Africans were part of a Spanish expedition to establish an outpost on the North American coast in present-day South Carolina.

1586   Scores of Africans plundered from the Spanish were aboard a fleet under the command of Sir Francis Drake when he arrived at Roanoke Island, Virginia.

1606   King James the First grants the first charter to the colony of Virginia, and it memorializes that the colony is bound by England's rule of law and the Magna Carta. Born in Virginia confers British subjecthood.

1616   Africans in the West Indies were at work in Bermuda, providing expert knowledge about tobacco cultivation.

1619   The first Africans are brought to Jamestown, Virginia, and other English colonies in America on the ship the *White Lion*. The Africans are treated as indentured servants, and after a defined period each is granted freedom and British subjecthood. Their children were born native sons of England.

1632   The colony of Maryland is granted a charter, and it memorializes that the colony is bound by England's rule of law and the Magna Carta. Born in Maryland confers British subjecthood.

1638   The New England slave trade begins in Boston.

1642   The beginning of the British Civil Wars. This pitted the supporters of King Charles I against the supporters of the Long Parliament.

1649   The execution of King Charles I.

1651   The end of the British Civil Wars.

1661   The colony of Virginia legalizes slavery in Virginia. The colonial law is void *ab initio* since slavery in Virginia violates Virginia's colonial charter. Virginia's governor succumbs to graft and corruption and fails to veto this law.

1662   The colony of Virginia enacts the law *partus sequitur ventrem*; chattel slavery. The colonial law is void *ab initio* since slavery at birth for children of slave women born in Virginia violates Virginia's colonial charter. Virginia's governor succumbs to graft and corruption and fails to veto this law.

1663   In Gloucester County, Virginia, the first documented slave rebellion in the American colonies takes place.

1663   The colony of Maryland legalized slavery.

1664   The colony of Maryland mandates lifelong servitude for all black slaves. Virginia, New York, New Jersey, and the Carolinas all pass similar laws.

1676   The colony of Virginia creates the "white race" in response to Bacon's

	Rebellion, where white and black colonials joined forces against British colonial rule.
1679	England's Parliament enacts the *Habeas Corpus Act of 1679*.
1682	Virginia declares that all imported black servants are slaves for life.
1689	England's Parliament enacts the *English Bill of Rights*. The bill codifies parliamentary sovereignty and liberty rights of all Englishmen. No Englishman can be born a slave.
1702	England's highest court rules in *Smith v. Browne & Cooper* that "as soon as a negro comes to England, he is free; one may be a villain in England, but not a slave."
1705	The *Virginia Slave Code* codifies slave status, declaring all non-Christian servants entering the colony to be slaves. It defines all slaves as real estate, acquits masters who kill slaves during punishment, forbids

slaves and free people of color from physically assaulting white persons, and denies slaves the right to bear arms or move abroad without written permission.

1708   The Southern colonies require militia captains to enlist and train one slave for every white soldier.

1708   Blacks outnumber whites in South Carolina.

1712   The *New York Slave Revolt of 1712*. Colonial America restricts the importation of Africans into the Colonies.

1729   The colonies of South and North Carolina are granted charters memorializing that the Magna Carta and English law binds the colony. Born in South and North Carolina conferred British subjecthood.

1732   The colony of Georgia is granted a charter, and it memorializes that the colony is bound by England's rule of law and the Magna Carta. Born in Georgia confers British subjecthood.

1735   Georgia petitions Britain's for the legalization of slavery.

1739   Slaves in Stono, South Carolina rebel, sacking and burning an armory and killing whites. The militia puts an end to the rebellion before slaves can reach freedom in Florida.

1751   King George II repeals *Virginia's Slave Code of 1705*.

1761   King George the Third marries Sophia Charlotte, daughter of Duke Charles Louis Frederick of Mecklenburg-Strelitz... Queen Charlotte. She's a direct descendant of the black branch of the Portuguese Royal House. Under America's Black Codes, she is black.

1762   Queen Charlotte gives birth to George the Fourth, who upon birth is named the Prince of Wales; the heir apparent to the British throne. Under Black Codes, he is black.

1766   Parliament passed the *Declaratory Act of 1766*. The Act abolished colonial proceedings by legislation, including colonial slave statutes and racialized hereditary slave laws, orders, and resolutions.

1770   Crispus Attacks, a black Englishman is the first person to die in Boston Massacre.

1771   England's highest court rules in *R. v. Stapylton* that being black will not prove ownership of a black person. The burden of proof belongs to the putative slave owner.

1772   England's highest court rules in *James Somerset v. Charles Stewart* that slavery was not "allowed and approved by the laws of this Kingdom" and grants freedom to a black native son. Slavery is deemed unconstitutional throughout the British Empire, and 15,000 native

America's First Big Lie

sons are immediately released from bondage in England and Wales.

1774   The First Continental Congress convenes in Philadelphia to organize colonial resistance to Parliament's Intolerable Acts passed in May of the same year and vows to discontinue the slave trade after December.

1775   Lord Dunmore, the governor of Virginia, declares martial law and conditionally grants freedom for all slaves held in bondage by colonial patriots.

1776   England's thirteen colonies declare themselves an independent nation and issue their *Declaration of Independence* in July. And Congress confers United States citizenship unto all free American colonists and formally adopts the English rule of law.

1779   England's General Henry Clinton issues The *Phillipsburg Proclamation* granting freedom to all Revolutionary War-era slaves and confers British subjecthood unto all Africans suffering as slaves in the Colonies.

1782   The United States sued for peace and entered the *Treaty of Paris of 1783*. England requires that all of its citizens be "set at liberty," and the United States agrees as a condition for peace. Hostilities cease.

1783   Waves of abuse were rampant. Black Englishmen are terrorized by slave catchers, and England files a formal complaint with the U. S. delegation, which includes George Washington. The delegation is informed that England takes the position that former slaves, particularly those born in colonial America, are Englishmen under his protection and that its practices must cease.

1783   General Guy Carleton transports 3,000 black native sons out of the

United States and memorializes their names in a *Book of Negroes*.

1784   Congress ratifies the *Definitive Treaty of Peace of 1783,* but failed to release 500,000 black Englishmen, relegates them to slavery claiming black Englishmen are legal property of white Americans. The United States violates its first international treaty.

1787   Delegates convenes a constitutional convention to draft a new federal United States Constitution.

1787   Congress reached a compromise to have an Electoral College and count black Englishmen as three-fifths of the number of white inhabitants of that state for legislative and taxing purposes.

1788   Congress ratifies the United States proslavery Constitution.

1790   Congress denies naturalization to anyone who is not a free white.

"[W]ho will tell the negro that he is free? Who will take him before [a] court to test the question of his freedom? In ignorance of his legal emancipation, he is kept..." Abraham Lincoln (circa 1854)

Chapter 1
Critical Race Theory

The U. S. Constitution is holy scripture for conservatives. Professional commentators on political and social matters writing in newspapers and magazines sometimes call this civil religion or civic religion. Conservatives are quick to claim the U. S. constitution is without error or fault in all teachings, whether related to ethics or the social, physical, or life sciences ... no different from the Bible. Conservatives' affinity to the constitution is the same as biblical inerrancy.

However, such reverence towards the proslavery U. S. Constitution is sadly misplaced when one considers that black colonials were legally free people. Parliament's *Declaratory Act of 1766* abolished colonial slave statutes and racialized colonial laws and regulations ten years before the Declaration of Independence in 1776, and there were no English laws that authorized slavery. Furthermore, colonial slavery was the product of colonial tyranny and was never a lawfully authorized practice under British law. The claim that slavery was lawful under "colonial statutes" is ahistorical and led to the disfranchisement and enslavement of 500,000 black colonials who were English citizens by law and entitled to be "set at liberty" by treaty. Enacting and ratifying a proslavery constitution was a fundamental and persisting question that the framers elected to accommodate for the Union to survive without considering the rule of law or the plight of black colonials.

The terms civil religion and civic religion refer to ritual expressions of patriotism. This is the underpinning of the fear conservatives have of teaching critical race theory in public schools. Among such practices of civil religion are crowds singing the national anthem at specific public gathering... parades or display of the national flag on certain patriotic holidays... reciting oaths of allegiance... ceremonies concomitant to the inauguration of a president or the coronation of a monarch... retelling exaggerated, one-sided, and simplified mythologized tales of national founders, great leaders or significant events... monuments commemorating great leaders of the past or historic events... monuments to dead soldiers or annual ceremonies to remember them... expressions of reverence for the state, the predominant national or racial group, the national constitution or monarch... expressions of solidarity with people perceived as being national kindred but residing in a foreign country or a foreign country perceived as being similar enough to the nation to warrant admiration and/or loyalty... expressions of hatred towards another country or foreign ethnic group perceived as either currently being an enemy of the state and/or as having wronged and slighted the nation in the past and public displays of the coffin of a recently deceased political leader.

Doubtlessly, for conservatives... the American Revolution produced a Moses-like leader in George Washington... prophets Thomas Jefferson and John Adams, and martyrs Crispus Attucks and Nathan Hale. Further, it created devils in King George III and Benedict Arnold...

as well as it produced sacred places like Valley Forge and Bunker Hill, and of course, emblems like the U. S. flag and a sacred holiday on the Fourth of July. And situated in the middle, serving as U. S. holy scripture, is the proslavery Constitution.

Conservatives see teaching critical race theory that interrogates, critiques, and exposes exaggerated, one-sided, and simplified mythologized tales of national founders, great leaders, significant events, and the U. S. constitution as an existential threat to this country. Further, Robert N. Bellah, in his article *Civil Religion in America,* observed that Thomas Jefferson was skeptical of this civil religious movement, writing in 1816… "some men look at constitutions with sanctimonious reverence and deem them like the Ark of the Covenant, too sacred to be touched." Jefferson knew then that this political orthodoxy was at odds with the ideals of the American Revolution and a multi-ethnic, multi-sectarian nation of people that America was conceived. Instead, continued protection of America's first big lie is the real problem. The existential threat to this nation is the continued reverence to a discredited dominant cultural narrative that black colonials were slaves or lesser Englishmen under the rule of law than white Englishmen based upon colonial statutes since it is anti-intellectual, promotes white supremacy and racial division.

Thus, there is a discordant debate about curricula and training sessions that teach racism is systemic and structural in America. However, teaching critical race theory is this nation's best opportunity to recalibrate this nation's core ideals of equality and democracy under the rule of law, expose the criminal enslavement of colonial blacks who were British citizens by law during the late 1780s and vanquish structural racism in a multi-ethnic and multi-sectarian nation. Forcing America's historiography toward truthful and honest accountings will be America's chickens coming home to roost since these ideals are immutable to a nation conceived in liberty and dedicated to the proposition that all men are created equal. Critical race theory (CRT) is a topical debate that will likely come to a local school board near you because it ruffles America's civil religion and constitutionalism.

In broad stroke... critical race theory attempts to demonstrate how racism continues to be a pervasive component throughout dominant society and why this persistent racism problematically denies individuals many of the constitutional freedoms they are otherwise promised in the United States' core governing documents: the Declaration of Independence and U. S. Constitution. Intricately connected to academic fields history, law, philosophy, and literature... CRT draws from works of writers like Frederick Douglass, Sojourner Truth, W.E.B. Dubois, James Baldwin, Dr. Martin Luther King Jr., and others tracing racism in America through the nation's legacy of slavery, racial terrorism, and *de jure* racial discrimination.

Critical race theory encompasses varied approaches such as storytellers who illustrate and explore lived experiences of racial oppression, structural determinism that explores how "the structure of legal thought or culture influences its content." And empathetic fallacy, believing that one can change a narrative by offering an alternative history, hoping that the recipient's empathy will quickly and reliably take over. But the threat to U. S. constitutionalism and America's civil religiosity is legitimate, as America's constitution is a proslavery document which CRT will critique how the social construction of race and institutionalized racism was codified and continues to perpetuate a racial caste system that relegates people of color to the bottom tiers. Further, CRT recognizes that race intersects with other identities, including sexuality, gender identity, and post-structuralism... developing in the mid-1970s with scholars like Derrick Bell, Alan Freeman, and Richard Delgado, who responded to what they identified as dangerously slow progress following the *Civil Rights Act of 1964*.

Conservatives have prevailed upon state and local governments to ban educators from teaching critical race theory in public schools. Eight states, South Carolina, Iowa, Arizona, Tennessee, New Hampshire, Texas, Oklahoma, and Idaho. These state laws ban the discussion, training, and orientation that the U. S. is inherently racist and any discussions about conscious and unconscious bias, privilege discrimination, and oppression.

The state school boards in Florida, Georgia, Utah, and Oklahoma adopted guidelines barring critical race theory-related discussions. All such laws and guidelines banning the teaching of critical race theory represent codified discrimination. They are violative of the *Civil Rights Act of 1964* as de *jure* discrimination can manifest itself by state laws of commission and omission. Further, all students have a First Amendment right to receive information and ideas… a privilege that most certainly applies in the context of school curriculum design. Moreover, public school educators have protection under the 14th Amendment that limits the authority of state and local governments to take away any benefit or privilege, including employment at a public school, for an arbitrary reason.

Those entrenched insiders in the conservative movement are not concerned that young white children might be taught that racism in America is systemic and structural. Instead, conservatives are deeply concerned that critical race theories will compromise U. S. constitutionalism and America's civil religion. Further, during the 1930s, Nazi Germany conferred international praise onto America's system of institutional racism and its civil religion. And although the government of America had a pre-World War II opportunity to denounce institutional racism and rebuff Nazi Germany's adulation… it did not. Instead, institutional racism and Jim Crow Laws were the norms in the U. S., and it radicalized an enthusiastic fan and devotee in the persona of Adolph Hitler. His praise for America's race laws was glowing and prominently highlighted in his book... *Mein Kampf.*

The U. S. leadership on a global level in *de jure* racism during the early twentieth century and its race laws fascinated the Germans, and it is well-documented. The *National Socialist Handbook for Law and Legislation of 1934-35*, edited by Hitler's lawyer Hans Frank, contains a seminal essay by Herbert Kier on the recommendations for race legislation which devoted a quarter of its pages to U. S. legislation... from race-based citizenship, segregation, immigration regulations, and anti-miscegenation. This directly inspired the *Nuremberg Laws*... Citizenship Law, and the Blood Law. At first, these defilement laws were aimed primarily at German Jews but were later extended to "Gypsies, Negroes and their bastard offspring." Ultimately, once World War II began... the Nazis grew the race defilement law to include all foreigners... non-Germans. These codified laws gave rise to the Holocaust and the loss of six million human lives whose only transgression was a racialized law based upon *de jure* U. S. laws.

Institutionalized racial segregation was ended as a government-endorsed practice in the U. S. during the civil rights movement by the efforts of such civil rights activists as Thurgood Marshall, Rosa Parks, James Farmer, and Rev. Dr. Martin Luther King, Jr., to name a few who worked for social and political freedom after the end of World War II. Happily, by 1968... all forms of segregation had been declared unconstitutional. Central to dissolving formal legal segregation in the United States was the Warren's court's decision in *Brown v. Board of Education of Topeka, Kansas* in 1954 outlawing segregation in public schools, and its decision in *Heart of Atlanta Motel, Inc. v. United States* prohibiting racial segregation and discrimination in public institutions and public accommodations. By using codified state laws to ban the teaching of the history of *de jure* segregation in America's public schools... conservatives are challenging the *Civil Rights Act of 1964*.

Conservatives find themselves in a quandary as they endeavor to craft a credible narrative to explain self-dealing by America's slaveholding founding generation and control damage to constitutionalism and America's civil religion. The revelation that the Framers of the constitution fashioned a proslavery document to enslave, exploit, and disfranchise 500,000 black Englishmen in violation of the rule of law will not only be seen as hypocrisy in calling themselves a

America's First Big Lie

beacon to human freedom, a *Shining City on the Hill*... it will have natural and foreseeable consequences for U. S. constitutionalism. Moreover, as the concealment of that which they seek to keep hidden becomes widely exposed and known, it eviscerates America's civil religion.

Teaching critical race theory is the nation's best hope of engaging young Americans in a frank, open, and evidence-based discussion of events, culture, and circumstances that led up to America's Revolutionary War. Relying on history's traditional role and by interrogating the role race played in the founding generation's handiwork, the Declaration of Independence... it can easily bear fruit in the future. Instead, continued allegiance to the notion of a faultless U. S. constitutional process and white supremacy dogma, without a thoughtful, engaged, and reasoned response to the stated indictments of racism, including, but not limited to colonial slavery being an extralegal institution, "colonial statutes" and racialized regulations being rendered void by Parliament's *Declaratory Act of 1766*, and England's high court ruling slavery was not "allowed and approved by the laws of this Kingdom" four years *before* the founding generation declared themselves independent of Great Britain during the mid-1770s can only rely upon a sycophantic reverence to America's discredited dominant cultural narrative.

The white supremacy narrative is peeling away... and commonsense dictates the teaching of critical race theory in schools is America's best chance to avert the looming possibility of social upheaval and catastrophic ramifications to U. S. constitutionalism. Moreover, it is the only way to recalibrate this nation's political trajectory, promote intellectualism and disabuse a nation of people of the taboos surrounding race in a multiethnic country.

History supports that reverence to English law was why the first 19 black people kidnapped from Africa were indentured servants, not slaves in colonial America in 1619. Everyone born in colonial America was an Englishman by birth, and no one was above or below English law. Teaching critical race theory would lead children and others to ask what changed English law to legalize colonial slavery if slavery was prohibited on British soil in 1619.

Further, Parliament's *Habeas Corpus Act of 1679* was directly connected to England's *Magna Carta of 1215*, clause 39, which barred colonial slavery. And teaching critical race theory will lead people to conclude that the practice of hereditary slavery was never approved or authorized within the colony of Virginia by English law, and colonial corruption caused colonial Virginia's lawgivers during the early 1660s to begin violating English law and Virginia's colonial charter.

Additionally, critical race theory recognizes that slavery was extralegal, the product of the corruption of colonial government during colonial rule... and the founding generation knew slavery was unlawful during British rule. The British imperial government's unofficial policy of salutary neglect and being three thousand miles away created colonial tyranny, racial terrorism, and hooliganism. Addressing the legality of slavery would lead children to understand that white privilege was a relic of a criminal scheme of enslaving colonial-born blacks and government corruption during colonial times. Without lawful authority.... colonial assemblies purported to enact colonial slave statutes and racialized regulations that enslaved legally free colonials and granted privileges to white colonials to shield the misanthrope practice that robbed black British citizens of their birthright of liberty. Moreover, hereditary slavery became a criminal act once the British imperial government recalibrated colonial affairs by passing the *Declaratory Act of 1766* that legislatively abolished colonial slave statutes, laws, orders, resolutions, and related racialized proceedings in "all cases whatsoever" and recalibrated the 13 colonial governments... ten years *before* the Declaration was adopted.

Furthermore, critical race theory will support the conclusion that the *Somerset* decision affirmed parliamentary sovereignty in 1772... and then judicially struck down colonial slave statutes, laws, votes, orders, and related regulations by ruling slavery as a practice was not "allowed and approved by the laws of this Kingdom." The *Somerset* decision established that slavery could only be a lawful condition in the Kingdom through a "positive law." Only Parliament had the lawful authority to enact a "positive law" during colonial times... and yet, *post*-America's Revolution erstwhile colonial slave masters such as George Washington, Thomas Jefferson, James Madison, and others claimed legal ownership of black Englishmen based upon colonial statutes and reduced them to be slaves in the United States without granting them due process, authorized by laws during the 1780s.

Doubly, the Framers of the U. S. Constitution then based its handiwork during the late 1780s upon this bare claim that colonial statutes were "positive laws" and were unaffected by the *Declaratory Act of 1766*, as well as the *Somerset* decision in 1772 and inexplicably, that colonial blacks were lawfully owned by white Americans as a run-up to the Declaration of Independence in 1776 and were not entitled to be "set at liberty" based upon their British citizenship under the *Definitive Treaty of Peace of 1783*.

History supports, America's founding generation, who self-described themselves as slave masters, did not own black colonials since slavery was never lawful on British soil, colonial assemblies could not enact a "positive law" to legalize slavery, and colonial slave statutes and racialized laws and regulations were rendered legal nullities by Parliament in 1766 and declared legal nullities by England's high court in 1772. Everyone living in the American colonies was a subject of King George III, and colonial-born blacks were countrymen of the founding generation and not slaves by English law. Black colonials held the same legal status, rights, and recourse under English law as the Patriots.

Lastly, in recognizing that the core criticism of teaching critical race theory in public schools that it leads to negative dynamics that divide people into "oppressed" and "oppressor" groups is a false, vacuous and disingenuous claim when one considers that the Fourth of July is a paid federal holiday and yet it too marks the day that 500,000 Revolutionary War-era blacks, although legally free people were placed *below* America's core governing document and were forced to become the bedrock of America's slave-based economy. These black colonials were free people in July 1776... since Parliament passed the *Declaratory Act of 1766* that repealed colonial slave statutes and racialized laws, regulations, resolutions. The *Somerset* decision struck down colonial slave statutes and laws in 1772 *before* adopting the Declaration of Independence on July 4, 1776.

Thus, critical race theory recognizes that the avoidance of this subject furthers structural racism, promotes ignorance, and adds to race taboos. After the American Revolution ended by treaty... the Continental Congress agreed to "set at liberty" all British citizens and confer U. S. citizenship unto British colonials that remained in the United States. Black colonials were Englishmen by law... and were entitled to liberty and U. S. citizenship if they remained in the United States. Yet, when the U. S. Constitution was ratified in the late 1780s, the Framers ignored the rule of law and, by fiat, enslaved 500,000 erstwhile black Englishmen and ratified a proslavery constitution. How the U. S. enslaved black colonials, who otherwise were U. S. citizens, and approved a constitution that promoted slavery and protected ownership of legally free black colonials compromises the U. S. Constitution.

History is the study of change over time, and it covers all aspects of human society. The political, social, economic, scientific, technological, medical, cultural, intellectual, religious, and military developments are part of history. Doubtlessly, structural racism is implicated in all aspects of human society... and it is a relic of white supremacy ideals... so banning teaching critical race theory in public schools is not the end game for conservatives.

The *Civil Rights Act of 1964* banned *de jure* racial segregation in public schools. Black legal scholars, academics, and students who spearheaded critical race theory in the early 1980s benefitted from this congressional act. And understandably, the cohort was responding to what they identified as dangerously slow progress following the *Civil Rights Act*. There and then... few if any had taken into real account the holding in the *Brown* case urging institutional discrimination be purged with "all deliberate speed." Fewer still knew that the U. S. Constitution was a proslavery document that made 500,000 legally free black Englishmen the bedrock of America's slave pool based upon defective codified laws and that the enslavement of black colonials violated the U. S. rule of law.

Abraham Lincoln observed this question in 1854 when he stated... "who will tell the negro that he is free? Who will take him before [a] court to test the question of his freedom? In ignorance of his *legal* emancipation, he is kept." Lincoln was more than likely referring to the legal emancipation of colonial blacks during British rule and the *Definitive Treaty of Peace of 1783*, where the U. S. government agreed to free all British citizens. Instead, the U. S. enslaved black British citizens based upon "colonial statutes," and it held the 13 states together during the constitutional convention in 1787.

The *Three-Fifths Compromise* was codified in the Constitution to avoid disunification. It centered around the disfranchisement of 500,000 black colonials who had U. S. citizenship by law and debate over the inclusion of these black colonials, who were reduced to slaves to measure a state's population for legislative and taxation purposes. Delegates from slaveholding states wanted black colonials to be fully counted for population purposes since everyone knew that they were *de facto* U. S. citizens. In contrast, representatives from non-slaveholding opposed counting them since slaveholding Americans claimed they were property and had no civil rights.

Moreover, the implication of this compromise is ever more troubling when one considers that nearly 95% of this black population was born in colonial America and was British citizens by birth. All colonial statutes and laws were rendered null and void for "all purposes whatsoever" under the *Declaratory Act of 1766*. And in the Declaration of Independence, there is a declarant noting that the British imperial government had abolished colonial laws and suspended colonial assemblies.

The actual legal status of the 500,000 black colonials reduced to slaves and disfranchised of U. S. citizenship during the late 1780s has provocative implications upon U. S. constitutionalism. By U. S. law, all Englishmen who stayed in the country automatically had U. S. citizenship due to their British citizenship. And if *de jure* colonial statutes that Americans claimed reduced them to slaves were legal nullities by Parliament's *Declaratory Act* and every delegate knew that this was the case... that would compromise the constitutional convention and resulting ratified constitution. History supports, colonial slave statutes and racialized colonial laws like *partus sequitur ventrem* were repealed by Parliament's *Declaratory Act of 1766*... ten years *before* the Declaration of Independence.

Hereditary slavery ceased being a legal practice during colonial times.

Further, colonial slave statutes and racialized hereditary laws and regulations were never legally promulgated, and colonial slavery was an extralegal practice. Moreover, the inherent defectiveness of colonial slave statutes and hereditary laws was given powerful affirmation when England's Court of the King's Bench in *James Somerset v. Charles Stewart* ruled slavery was not "allowed and approved by the laws of this Kingdom" and struck down "colonial statutes" in 1772. Then four years later... the founding generation famously claimed King George III's imperial government had indeed abolished colonial laws and assemblies in the Declaration of Independence in July 1776... claiming it was tyranny. And yet, at the end of America's Revolutionary War... America's Constitution legitimated slavery and protected slaveholding Americans.

The U. S. Constitution is a proslavery document, and America's slaveholding Patriots controlled the constitutional convention. It is a well-settled fact that disunification of the 13 states was the overarching concern of the delegates... slaveholding American James Madison and his cohort changed the ground rules of the convention, and the Constitution has protected their facile ownership claims and promoted the practice of slavery. Liberal rumblings are pushing for a constitutional convention... and conservatives are fearful of that prospect. Conservatives believe that if "colonial statutes" are revealed as being lawfully repealed by Parliament's *Declaratory Act of 1766*... struck down by England's Court of the King's Bench in 1772... and the Declaration of Independence confirms the abolishment of colonial slave statutes during British rule... America's constitution will become a hopelessly compromised document. This perspective is given powerful reaffirmation by the *Heritage Foundation*, a conservative organization. They appear to endorse the view that critical race theory "[W]hen followed to its logical conclusion, CRT is destructive and rejects the fundamental ideas on which our constitutional republic is based."

The *Heritage Foundation's* view of the implications of teaching critical race theory is not too dramatic. Washington's "colonial statute" claim was used to justify enslaving 500,000 black colonials after the American Revolution. Proving "colonial statutes" were null and void based upon the actions of the British imperial government in 1766 would mean white slaveholding Patriots such as Washington, Thomas Jefferson, James Madison, John Marshall, and others did not own these black Englishmen. Moreover, it would mean slaveholding Americans were criminals under British rule. America's dominant cultural narrative regarding the dogma of white supremacy and slavery would collapse, as does America's proslavery constitution.

The American Revolution of the mid-1770s was a British civil war waged by Englishmen in North America against their mother country, Great Britain. Further, the United States did not win the American Revolution. Instead, this nation sued for peace in 1782, and the civil war ended with the ratification of the *Definitive Treaty of Peace 1783*. And by treaty, the U. S. government was obligated to "set at liberty" the 500,000 black Englishmen living in colonial America. However, the U. S. enslaved them and denied them due process.

Doubtlessly, ethnic black Englishmen lived in colonial America, and colonial slavery was an extralegal institution. Born in colonial America made that person an Englishmen. Black colonials were suffering under a regime of colonial governmental tyranny, racial terrorism, and hooliganism when the British imperial government abolished colonial slave statutes, laws, and racialized regulations and recalibrated the colonial government by the *Declaratory Act of 1766*. Thus, it is not a fair characterization to claim that the United States is a nation of immigrants.

The text of the U. S. Constitution is proslavery, as the document contains eleven clauses that dealt with or had policy implications for slavery. Ten clauses protected slave property and irrefutably confirming racism is "systemic" and structurally embedded in America's legal system and institutions, critical race theory's core assertion. For example, the *Apportionment Clause*, Article I, Section 2, commonly referred to as the Three-Fifths Compromise, added three-fifths of "all other Persons" (slaves) to the number of free inhabitants of a state for purposes of representation. By boosting the number of representatives in Congress for the slave states, this clause guaranteed political protection for slavery. The same three-fifths ratio increased the representation of slave states in the Electoral College during presidential elections. However, slavery was not a lawful institution under British rule, colonial slave statutes were rendered null and void by Parliament's *Declaratory Act of 1766*, and these so-called "slaves" were, in reality, U. S. citizens due to their British citizenship and entitled to be fully counted.

Further, the slave import limitation, Article I, Section 9, prohibited Congress from regulating the international slave trade, but Article V of the Constitution explicitly forbids amending the slave import limitation... one of only two such forbidden matters in the whole document. Moreover, the *Fugitive Slave Clause*, Article IV, Section 2, guaranteed nationally for the first time the right of slave owners to pursue and reclaim their slaves anywhere throughout the land. This way... if black colonials were free Englishmen and not property by the rule of law... an insurmountable problem is created for constitutionalism and white supremacists.

The fact that colonial statutes were null and void under the *Declaratory Act of 1766*... colonial blacks' legal status and rights were returned to status *quo ante* once England's Court of the King's Bench struck down colonial slave statutes in 1772. The Declaration of Independence proclaimed "all men are created equal" is another reason conservatives are afraid of critical race theories in public schools. Constitutional scholar John Hart Ely believed that "strict constructionism" is not a philosophy of law or a theory of interpretation but a coded label for judicial decisions popular with a particular party. This conclusion is supported by the fact that critics who oppose teaching critical race theories are not found clamoring that critical race theory teachings create problems for constitutionalism ... instead, they advance the argument that critical race theory teaches white children to hate their country and intolerance.

Blaming the controversy on concerns for children is a diversionary tactic on the part of conservatives when one considers their robust and historical embracement of strict constructionism and their inability to defend America's dominant cultural narrative that declares black Englishmen were the slaves of white Americans based upon "colonial statutes." Further, conservatives have long supported a strictly literal interpretation of the constitution and then looking towards legislative intent to interpret the constitutional provisions. They do not want a scholarly debate on the proslavery question. Nonetheless, their stated speaking points have found their way into the public education discourse and require a response, as constitutions are not just about restraining and limiting power. Instead, constitutions are about fidelity to the rule of law and the empowerment of ordinary people in a democracy and allowing them to control government sources to their aspirations. However, the soft underbelly of the philosophy of U. S. constitutionalism is that the constitution is a proslavery document, and the demonstrable intent of the Framers of this document was to place certain people above the rule of law and to further their criminal practice of enslavement and exploitation of legally free black people.

Thus, in a nutshell... conservative critics are afraid of critical race theory because of the potential consequences to U. S. constitutionalism and damage to its coveted self-image of being an exceptional nation when it becomes an accepted fact that black colonials were not slaves here in America based upon "colonial statutes" and the U. S. government codified racial discrimination to legitimized enslaving and exploiting free people in derogation of its own rule of law.

"It is certain, in any case, that ignorance, allied with power, is the most ferocious enemy justice can have." James A. Baldwin

Chapter 2
Hypocritical Race Theory

The best way to label conservatives who oppose teaching critical race theory is to call them hypocritical race theorists. They are committed to mythology instead of American history. History is the study of change over time, and it covers all aspects of human society. The political, social, economic, scientific, technological, medical, cultural, intellectual, religious, and military developments are part of history. Further, history supports that black colonials existed in colonial America... were legally free people under the British rule of law... had a role in the run-up to the American Revolution... were British citizens by law when the founding generation adopted the Declaration of Independence in 1776 and were all entitled to be "set at liberty" under the *Definitive Treaty of Peace of 1783*... yet, were unlawfully detained here in America and made the bedrock of America's slave-based economy and have participated in all aspects of human society in America. However, conservatives do not want such things taught in public schools and are resolved to ban critical race theory by enacting a *de jure* discrimination law.

The *Civil Rights Act of 1964* prohibits segregation and discrimination based upon race in public schools. Thus, the threshold challenge of enacting state laws banning public school educators from teaching critical race theory is the *Civil Rights Act* since the role, existence, and contributions of so-called black colonials during British rule and then blacks in America *after* adopting the Declaration of Independence on July 4, 1776... is orthodox U. S. history.

Doubtlessly, under the rule of law, discrimination can be accomplished, like any other misdeed by commission and omission. Thus, state school and local boards could not lawfully delete, alter, or sanitize a U. S. history curriculum with the selective exclusion of blacks, native Americans, and race-related events and call such a curriculum U. S. history. Further, in the 1974 case *Lau v. Nichols*, the Supreme Court ruled that the San Francisco school board violated non-English speaking students' rights under the 1964 act by placing them in regular classes rather than providing some accommodation. Moreover, the law authorized the Department of Justice to sue local school boards to end allegedly discriminatory practices.

History supports, the U. S. was a multi-racial nation when created in the year 1776. Black colonials were Englishmen under the British rule of law. The legal status of the first nineteen or twenty kidnapped Africans arriving on Virginia's shores in 1619 were indentured servants... not slaves. Colonial statutes and laws authorizing slavery were colonial tyranny due to corruption of colonial government and racial terrorism. The British imperial government abolished colonial statutes and racialized laws and regulations through Parliament's *Declaratory Act of 1766*. Six years later... colonial slave statutes were struck down by England's Court of the King's Bench in 1772. Colonial America's institutional racism was nullified completely four years *before* the Declaration of Independence. Black colonials were equal to white Englishmen under the English rule of law in 1776 and fought alongside white patriots for independence from British rule in the resulting *American Revolution*. These things are well-settled by historical records and cannot be seriously contested by historians.

The opposition to teaching critical race theory is at best, a collateral attack upon the *Civil Rights Act of 1964*. The selective expungement and alteration of U. S. historiography to promulgate white nationalist mythology... is *per se* discriminatory. Yet, conservative critics do have support and advocates within state legislatures who have enacted laws or have ones pending that will ban teaching critical race theory within the context of teaching U. S. history that seeks to erase or mischaracterize the integral role, existence, and significant contributions made by people of color in America's origin and development as a superpower. These state laws violate the *Civil Rights Act of 1964*. They are being enacted to idealize racist, discredited, and ahistorical views of U. S. history and race relations in America. The state laws violate the *Act of 1964* as they further discrimination in schools based upon race.

In *Brown v. Board of Education* (1954) 347 U. S. 483, attorneys for the NAACP referred to the phrase "equal but separate" used in *Plessy v. Ferguson* as a custom de jure racial segregation enacted into law. The NAACP was successful in challenging the constitutional viability of the *"separate but equal"* doctrine. The Warren Court declared:

> "... in the field of public education, the doctrine of "separate but equal" has no place. Separate educational facilities are inherently unequal. Therefore, we hold that the plaintiffs and others similarly situated for whom the

actions have been brought are, by reason of the segregation complained of, deprived of the equal protection of the laws guaranteed by the Fourteenth Amendment."

The *Brown* decision outlawed segregated public education facilities for blacks and whites at the state level. The companion case of *Bolling v. Sharpe*, 347 U. S. 497 outlawed such practices at the Federal level in the District of Columbia.

The nationwide initiative to ban teaching critical race theory in public schools is *de jure* discrimination. These laws enacted by various state legislatures embody the same anti-intellectual... white supremacist ideals and directly attack the *Civil Rights Act of 1964* that outlawed discriminatory practices based upon race, color, religion, sex, or national origin. The enactment of laws banning teaching critical race theory by state governments violates the 14th Amendment and can have a disparate impact on school-aged students of color within public schools. Further, laws banning teaching critical race represent censorship. As it is a white chauvinistic perspective of U. S. history forced upon all students in public schools, it cannot be sanctioned since this nation was always multi-racial, slavery violated the rule of English law, and such censorship will harden institutional racism within public schools and beyond... as black colonials were reduced to chattel property in violation of the British rule of law and then passed laws that institutionalized racism.

For example... Crispus Attucks was the first to fall during the *Boston Massacre* in 1770... the first casualty of the American Revolution. He was an Englishman by his birth as Attucks was born sometime around 1723 in Framington, Massachusetts. Moreover, Attucks has been celebrated as one of the first martyrs in the fight for American independence and symbolizes the black colonial struggle for freedom and equality. Attucks' father was an enslaved African, and his mother, a Native American. And as a symbol of resistance to tyranny, Attucks death placed him among the immortals. Today his name tops the names of the five carved in the monument of granite and bronze erected to commemorate that historic night in Boston Commons in 1770. Yet, Attucks' contribution to America's cause for independence and other black colonials can be eviscerated from being taught in public schools for no other reason but their race and ethnicity based upon laws enacted at the state and local governmental levels.

But two generations ago... Rev. Dr. Martin Luther King wrote in his book... "Why We Cannot Wait" that children, especially black children, needed to "know that the first

American to shed blood in the revolution that freed his country from British oppression was a Black seaman named Crispus Attucks." Doubtlessly, portended state and local laws that ban teaching critical race theory in public schools are weapons conservatives are using to forestall and prevent children from learning the role Attucks' death played in the run-up to America's adoption of the Declaration of Independence.

State and local laws that ban teaching critical race theory to children in public schools because of its likely impact upon white children... even if this was a real concern, constitute censorship. Further, teaching curricula that intentionally remove critical race teachings out of America's historiography cannot be deemed U. S. history. Such curricula would have to be differently named as history is the study of change over time, and it covers all aspects of human society. These state and local laws banning the teaching of critical race theory are symbolic of a harsh and oppressive regime seeking to censor and silence prevailing black culture.

Moreover, by inference... such state and local laws proclaim that white children's emotional and mental health is more worthy of protection by school boards than black children's emotional and mental health. This is invidiously racist and undermines the guarantee to all citizens of equal protection of the laws through the 14th Amendment of the United States Constitution. These state and local laws are improvidently using "race" as a determinative for deciding public school curricula.

America's actual historiography becoming known by educators... being greenlit to be taught in public schools to children is forcing parents to deal with three threshold questions. First, did "colonial statutes" have the legal sufficiency to enslave 500,000 British citizens *after* the *Definitive Treaty of Peace of 1783* ended the American Revolution, and if not, why not. Second, did the U. S. violate due process rights when it failed to grant habeas corpus hearings to the 500,000 black colonials that its American citizens enslaved, exploited, and disfranchised during the 1780s. Third, is the U. S. Constitution a proslavery document enacted to protect slavery and promote slave ownership?

Framed as threshold questions... proffered as the hidden reasoning upon which conservative critics on the Right oppose the teaching of critical race theory... "colonial statutes" were legal nullities since they never were lawfully promulgated and then repealed by the *Declaratory Act of 1766*. History supports that slavery was a criminal practice when the 13 colonies declared themselves a new nation in 1776. The British imperial government rendered colonial statutes "utterly null and void for all purposes whatsoever" in 1766, ten years earlier. Consequently, there was absolutely no legal sufficiency to justify enslaving the 500,000 black colonials *after* the *Definitive Treaty of Peace of 1783* ended the American Revolution based upon "colonial statutes."

Second, the U. S. adopted English law *after* adopting the Declaration of Independence in July 1776. The Continental Congress's adoption of English law... bound this new nation to the *Magna Carta of 1215* and Anglo-Saxon jurisprudence and traditions. Liberty was a personal right during colonial times. Thus, even if white colonials' putative ownership of black colonials had not been rendered null and void by the *Declaratory Act of 1766*... the slaveholding Patriots were legally required to prove their claims of ownership of the black colonials under *R. v. Stapylton* (K.B. 1771) ("being black will not prove the property.")

Third, America's Constitution protected slavery and promoted slave ownership. The *Apportionment Clause,* Article I, Section 2 added three-fifths of "all other Persons" ...slaves... to the number of free inhabitants for representation purposes. By boosting the number of representatives in Congress for the slave states, this clause guaranteed political protection for slavery.

The same three-fifths ratio increased the representation of slave states in the *Electoral College* during presidential elections that delivered the presidency to Thomas Jefferson in 1800. The slave import limitation, Article I, Section 9, prohibited Congress from regulating the international slave trade until 1808, 21 years after the ratification of the Constitution. Not only was Congress forbidden from regulating the transoceanic slave trade, but Article V of the Constitution explicitly forbids amending the slave import limitation, one of only two such forbidden matters in the whole document.

Lastly, the *Fugitive Slave Clause*, Article IV, Section 2, guaranteed nationally, for the first time, the right of slave owners to pursue and reclaim their slaves anywhere throughout the land is proslavery. Ultimately, it took a Civil War and constitutional amendments to eliminate slavery. However, racial repression, white supremacy, and inequality can be traced back to slavery throughout American history and persist today.

The Constitution thus protected slavery by increasing political representation for slave owners and slave states, limiting, although temporarily, congressional power to regulate the international slave trade, and by protecting the rights of slave owners to recapture erstwhile black colonials who escaped and sought freedom. The Constitution also promoted slave ownership by delivering increased political representation while keeping the flow of slaves unregulated through the international slave trade for 21 years. And due to the political environment, in its absence of a *locus classicus* or a reparations study bill or the like, all too many will forever believe any proposed curative relief by the U. S. government is wasteful and undeserving. In contrast, others… many of whom are hereditary stakeholders, will never be satisfied.

There is an Anglo-Saxon jurisprudence maxim: *"for every right, there is a legal remedy, where there is no remedy, there is no right."* There are two categories of remedies: a legal remedy for a legal right and an equitable remedy for other rights. The Continental Congress formally adopted English law in July 1776, which means America's legal system was founded upon Anglo-Saxon jurisprudence traditions.

Further, early America's legal system had two distinct types of courts… courts of law and courts of equity. And by design, remedies must be decided *after* the complaining party can present sufficient evidence that they suffered a legal wrong or are permitted to set forth facts and circumstances justifying equitable relief. And in all instances, there must be underlying facts and evidence supporting any remedy granted. Unfortunately, this has yet to occur.

The U. S. government advanced and protected a false narrative that enslaving 500,000 black colonials after the American Revolution was lawful based upon "colonial statutes" to rob black people of fundamental legal rights and wealth. Their descendants are the real-party-interest who have been underrepresented in the restorative justice discussion. The proper remedy for enslaving black colonials is restitution... not reparations. Legal remedies matter. Reparations for black slavery shred the constitutional logic of a fair, impartial justice system.

The Fourth of July is an annualized national holiday for reckoning America's core idea of equality of citizenship. This is the first Fourth of July in the wake of Juneteenth becoming a national holiday and is an auspicious time to reimagine America's Declaration of Independence, as well as Frederick Douglass's speech... *What to the Slave is the Fourth of July*?

Plucked into the middle of a national discourse about the teaching of critical race theory in public schools, Juneteenth became a national holiday because of critical race theory. This is its best testamentary evidence. Douglass's *pre*-Civil War speech exploring racial injustice and the broken promise of equality and liberty under the rule of law announced in the Declaration of Independence during the 1850s is particularly relevant for the times. Douglass, a former slave, made the thoughtful observation to an audience of nearly 600 that "This Fourth of July is yours, nor mines. You may rejoice, I must mourn."

Doubtlessly, America's Declaration of Independence was the product of grievance politics triggered by England's Court of the King's Bench's unanimous ruling in the *James Somerset v. Charles Stewart* habeas case in 1772 that freed Somerset and proclaimed slavery was not "allowed and approved by the laws of this Kingdom." Parliament's exercise of its supreme legislative power, parliamentary sovereignty by way of the *Declaratory Act of 1766,* had already rendered colonial slave statutes in the American colonies "utterly null and void for all purposes for whatsoever" six years earlier. This judicial decision by England's highest court was controlling precedent that struck down colonial slave statutes and laws and reaffirmed that slavery within the Kingdom could only be a legal condition if enacted by a "positive law" passed by the British Parliament.

Belatedly, the British imperial government recognized that in allowing a vast swart of colonials to do things against colonials of color in derogation of the rule of law, the colonial government had weakened the core principle of equality under the rule of law that underpinned England's *Magna Carta of 1215*. Among its many provisions, one of the most important is the proposition that no person should be deprived of their liberty or property "except by the lawful judgement of his equals or by the law of the land"... colonial slavery was a not lawful condition within the 13 American colonies when the Continental Congress adopted the Declaration of Independence on July 4, 1776.

Essentially, Douglass's Fourth of July speech criticized his audience's boundless pride for a nation that claimed to value freedom and allegiance to the rule of law. Yet, the founders created a regime of slavery in the United States. Douglass found the claim that slavery was inherited from British rule to be feckless and disingenuous when juxtaposed to the notion that America was built upon the idea of liberty, freedom, and the rule of law... not men. Still, Douglass tells his audience that more than anything... America is built upon uncontested claims, legal inconsistencies, and hypocrisies that have been overlooked for so long they appear to be truths. Moreover, as a threshold to understanding Douglass's truism... one must first understand that America's Revolutionary war was a civil war. Black colonials fought on both sides and were British citizens by law.

Further, Douglass muses that we do not celebrate the Fourth because it is the day that the founding fathers declared independence from England, as that was accomplished through an act of the Continental Congress two days prior, on July 2. Instead, we celebrate the Fourth because it is the day the Continental Congress adopted the Declaration of Independence. Further, America's independence from England came with the *Definitive Treaty of Peace of 1783* on January 14, 1784.

In a run-up to the American Revolution... all vestiges of slavery, white colonial privileges, and race-based regulations that placed black colonials *below* the rule of English law within colonial America were legislatively abolished by the British imperial government and *Parliament's Declaratory Act of 1766*. Those colonial ruling-class statutes, laws, orders, and regulations had established and were sustaining slavery and white colonial supremacy. And the British imperial government abolished all unearned privileges and status granted unto white colonials in 1766 by parliamentary sovereignty. This enactment by Parliament caused a recalibration of colonial governance by nullifying all repugnant colonial legislative proceedings and returned black colonials to status *quo ante*. Thus, by recognizing that the *Declaratory Act of 1766* abolished colonial slave statutes and racialized regulations and England's highest court affirmed that slavery was not a lawful condition in the Kingdom in the *Somerset* decision in 1772… that the Declaration's equality provision did include black colonials as a matter of law when one takes in account all five sections of the Declaration of Independence.

Doubtlessly, the Declaration of Independence's grievance section is condemnatory of King George III and the British Parliament for passing the *Declaratory Act of 1766*… "**He has combined with others to subject us to jurisdiction foreign to our constitution and unacknowledged by our laws, giving his assent to their Acts of pretended Legislation**"… "**For taking our Charters, abolishing our most valuable Laws, and altering fundamentally the Forms of our Governments.**" Slavemasters in colonial America knew colonial statutes were abolished and could no longer rely upon deferential colonial

America's First Big Lie

government officials to protect them. The British imperial government eviscerated the colonial slavery scheme by abolishing repugnant racialized colonial laws with Parliament's *Declaratory Act of 1766*.

Further, the British imperial government's exercise of parliamentary sovereignty in 1766 destroyed the ability of colonial slavemasters to safely claim ownership of black colonials based upon "colonial statutes,"... even if the King had previously permitted it. Then in 1772... England's Court of the King's Bench declared slavery was not "allowed and approved by the laws of this Kingdom." This King's Bench decision turned colonial slavery within the American colonies into a criminal enterprise.

In the *Somerset* case, England's King's Bench ruling disabused all slave-holding citizens within the American colonies of slavery's legality in 1772. Yet, few slave-holding Englishmen within the American colonies released the black citizens they were criminally exploiting as slaves. Sadly, none of these slaveholding colonials were held to account by the colonial government. And yet, revisionist historians claim slave-holding colonials hated slavery. It is claimed that Jefferson called slavery a "hideous blot" on America. And George Washington, who owned hundreds of slaves, denounced it as "repugnant."

Yet, Jefferson went on to have carnal relations and fathered children with a twelve-year-old colonial-born black child named Sally Hemings. While Washington's dentures were teeth belonging to black colonials, which he called slaves even *after* colonial slave statutes were repealed due to the *Declaratory Act of 1766* and even after slavery was declared as not being "allowed and approved by the laws of this Kingdom" in the *Somerset* decision in 1772.

After the *Declaratory Act of 1766*... the attitude of slaveholding colonials toward the mother country became isolationism, hostile to humanitarianism, and defiant of the rule of English law. And, yet in July 1776... the slaveholding Americans formally adopted the English rule of law to govern this new nation. They joined with northern colonials and rejected a bill to adopt Roman law led by Thomas Jefferson. And a compelling, dispositive fact is revealed by looking at the congressional records debating this issue in July 1776.

First, the Patriots knew black colonials were not slaves, and those colonial statutes had been abolished by the British imperial government's *Declaratory Act of 1766* and the *Somerset* decision in 1772. As a congressional proponent of Roman law explained, "Roman law offers this new republic an opportunity to develop a particular American jurisprudence, which would not be just a slavish imitator of the English common law that is hostile to many a man's interest here in this hall."

Second, the Congressional hearing regarding Jefferson's Roman Law bill in 1776 was full-throated. The legislators were fully advised in the premise and propriety of this new law… and Congress was not persuaded. As a result, Congress rejected Jefferson's bill to adopt Roman law that would have legalized *partus sequitur ventrem* in the future. Instead, Congress formally adopted the English rule of law that embraced the due process of law… the same rule of law that transformed captive Africans into indentured servants in 1619.

Further, Jefferson forever complained that Congress had "mangled" the Declaration of Independence. Jefferson's complaint is self-evident when one understands that the U. S. did later ratify a proslavery constitution that approved enslaving legally free black colonials and protected slaveholding Americans.

Third, the British imperial government caused slavemasters to oppose King George III's governance in the Declaration of Independence's "For taking our Charters, abolishing our most valuable Laws and altering fundamentally the Forms of our Governments." The King's Bench ruled slavery was not "allowed and approved by the laws of this Kingdom" in the 1772 *Somerset* case.

Doubtlessly, congressional records of the historical debate to supplant English law with Roman law during the summer of 1776 is dispositive proof that the Framers of the new federal constitution in 1787 knew that black colonials were legally free people with varied legal rights under the English rule of law.

Stripped of all vestiges of devolved power, colonial assemblies and their former legislators in the run-up to the Declaration did not have legislative power, real or imagined, to unilaterally enact a positive law authorizing slavery or to strip a colonial-born person of British subjecthood. The imperial government's suspension of colonial assemblies and the absence of plenary power explains why the Declaration of Independence's pronouncement that "all men are created equal" did not and could not carve out black colonials.

Moreover, in the Declaration of Independence's preamble... the word freedom comes right after equality. It was embryonic in America's founding creed of equality, as the *"Shining City on a Hill"* was supposed to replace a remote, British imperial government. "State a moral case to a ploughman and a professor." Thomas Jefferson wrote in 1787. "The former will decide it as well, and often better than the latter because he has not been led astray by artificial rules." Moral equality was the basis for political equality. Yet, for generations, the U. S. backed up its self-anointed claim of exceptionalism by its proslavery Constitution.

The dominant cultural narrative has portrayed slavery's insinuation in America as being lawful. This was untrue. The founding generation's core grievance with British imperial governance was Parliament's *Declaratory Act of 1766* abolished colonial slave statutes. The King was withholding his assent to all new laws passed by colonial assemblies. Further, four years *before* the Declaration of Independence, the *Somerset* decision struck down slave laws within the American colonies. The American colonies were part of King George III's kingdom in 1772. The British imperial court ruled slavery had to be authorized in the Kingdom by "positive law." The slave practices in colonial America were not exempted.

Black colonials could not be slaves based upon "colonial statutes." The black colonials should have been "set at liberty" at the end of the

American Revolution. Moreover, the men who became the founding fathers were confident that those suffering as slaves would accept anything their white masters told them. And even though George Washington's "colonial statutes" claim was facile and could not legitimate enslaving 500,000 black colonials... they did little to shore up the feckless claim since the U. S. had a proslavery constitution.

Further, untangling the criminal scheme of the slaveholding Americans required accurate facts, critical thinking skills, and the careful analysis of historical evidence. But, the slaveholding Patriots and their descendants were totally at ease as they were tirelessly committed to disinformation and, due to this tactic and passage of time, came to say that "if you want to hide something from a nigger, just put it in a book."

"Those who have no record of what their forebears have accomplished lose the inspiration which comes from the teaching of biography and history." Carter G. Woodson

Chapter 3
America's True Legacy

Colonial slave statutes were legal fictions, as a matter of English law, since slavery was not authorized on British soil and colonial assemblies did not have the legal authority to enact a "positive law" that authorized colonial slavery. Further, colonial slavery was a criminal practice... the product of corrupt colonial governance and was repugnant to English law. England's *Magna Carta* of 1215, Parliament's *Habeas Corpus Act of 1679,* and common law had long declared "one may be a villien in England, but not a slave." The protections and birthrights conferred unto native sons of England began in the 13th century... over four hundred years *before* the first recorded person of African ancestry ever arrived upon British soil during the late 16th century. No one was above or below English law, and no Englishman could be born a slave.

Blacks born in colonial North America were Englishmen by birth. They were deemed "children of the King" protected by a 1350 "**statute for those who are born in Parts beyond Sea.**" Further, as provided in Virginia's colonial charter of 1606 and each of the twelve additional colonial charters, in relevant part...

> "Also we do, for Us, our Heirs, and Successors, DECLARE, by these Presents, that all and every the Persons being our Subjects, which shall dwell and inhabit within every or any of the said several Colonies and Plantations, and every of their children, which shall happen to be born within any of the Limits and Precincts of the said Colonies and Plantations, shall HAVE and enjoy all Liberties, Franchises, and Immunities, within any of our other Dominions, to all Intents and Purpose, as if they had been abiding and born, within this our Realm of England, or any other of our Dominions."

English law was why the first 19 black people kidnapped from Africa were indentured servants, not slaves, in 1619. This was not by luck... instead, slavery was not approved or authorized within the colony of Virginia by English law, and colonial Virginia's lawgivers were adhering to English law and its colonial charter... no one was above or below English law. The *Habeas Corpus Act of 1679* was directly connected to England's *Magna Carta of 1215*, clause 39, which colonial slavery violated.

In being a government of laws, not men, the colony of Virginia meant that the first Africans, after serving their terms as indentured servitude, fell into a well-established socio-economic system. Virginia's socio-economic system reflected no racism or repression. For example, Anthony Johnson was one of the first Africans to arrive in colonial Virginia. After serving as an indentured servant until 1635, he became free and a significant property owner... owning 250 acres of fertile land and holding five indentured servant contracts by 1651.

Johnson married an African named Isabelle. She gave birth to their son William in 1623 or 1624... the first recorded Afro-Englishman born in the colonies and no different from today in the U. S., born in colonial America, conferred birthright citizenship. However, in 1652, "an unfortunate fire" caused "great losses" for Johnson. He applied to the colonial court for tax relief. Without regard to Johnson's African origins, the colonial court not only reduced his taxes, evidencing that kidnapped Africans who became free British subjects had rights under England's common law in early colonial America but, surprisingly, Virginia's rule of lawgivers even exempted Johnson's wife and his two minor daughters from paying a tax "during their natural lives."

During this time, taxes were levied on people, not property, as Virginia's *1645 Taxation Act* provided: "All negro men and women and all other men from the age of 16 to 60 shall be tithable." The colonial court's exemption of Johnson's wife and daughters from the obligation to pay taxes gave them the same exempt status and rights of freeborn white women, who were not taxed in colonial Virginia.

Then in 1654... in a civil case in colonial Virginia titled *Anthony Johnson v. Robert Parker*, this kidnapped African prevailed against a white colonist in a replevin case involving John Casor, a black indentured servant whose contract was owned by Johnson, but... had been transferred to Parker with no valuable consideration. Casor had complained to Parker that his indentured contract had expired seven years earlier and that he was being held in an illegal state of servitude. Parker intervened on behalf of Casor and cajoled Johnson into releasing him since keeping indentured servants past the expiration of their term of servitude was a heinous offense. An offending party could be severely punished for such an offense. However, Johnson, who was illiterate, brought a lawsuit once he discovered that he'd been tricked by Parker, as Casor signed a term of indenture to Parker. Afterward, Johnson sought the nullification of his release and the return of Casor.

Initially, the colonial court ruled in favor of Parker, but Johnson appealed the decision, and in 1655, the ruling was reversed. The higher court found in favor of this black colonist Johnson, and it nullified Johnson's release and directed Parker to return Casor and pay court fees immediately. In sustaining Johnson's cause of action against Parker, the verdict established that black colonists and foreign-born people of African ancestry could bring lawsuits in colonial times and prevail under the English rule of law.

Without much dispute, Johnson securing tax relief in 1652 and the favorable disposition of his 1654 civil case against a white colonist to recover ownership of an indentured servant contract are significant because they do establish a treatment and normal social status accorded to people of African ancestry who became Englishmen and subjects of the King… a treatment and status that was practically and theoretically incompatible with a system of racial repression or structural racism.

In the early 1640s, a series of civil wars erupted between Royalists and Parliamentarians. Great Britain was "a nation of laws, not men," and "no one was above or below English law." However, England's monarch, King Charles I, believed in the *Divine Right of Kings*. This ideology was opposed by those who thought there should be a limit to Royal authority. The people and their representatives believed Parliament should have more say in how the nation was governed. Tied up with this were arguments over the Church and religion. This led to the *English Civil Wars* and *Glorious Rebellion...* 1642 through 1688. During this period, the extralegal institution of colonial slavery developed and hardened.

The Parliamentarians won the civil wars, which led to the English monarchy's replacement with the Commonwealth of England under Oliver and Richard Cromwell. Constitutionally, the actions established the precedent that an English monarch cannot govern without Parliament's consent. And the principle of parliamentary sovereignty or supremacy was legally established as part of the *Glorious Revolution* in 1688. The following year, Parliament codified parliamentary sovereignty in the *English Bill of Rights of 1689*. The parliamentary sovereignty principle holds that this legislative body has absolute authority and is supreme over all other government institutions within the Kingdom, including executive and judicial bodies.

Elizabeth Key is the who behind hereditary slavery. Key was born in 1630 in Warwick County, Virginia, to an indentured African woman. Her white father, Thomas Key, was born in England, and he came to Virginia in 1616 and was considered a pioneer tobacco planter. He was elected to Virginia's legislative assembly, the House of Burgesses, representing Warwick County.

The wealthy Key denied paternity, a court proceeding followed, and he was ordered to take responsibility for her. Under English law, fathers were obligated to care for their children, even if they were illegitimate. Key then took responsibility for Elizabeth, arranging for her baptism in the Church of England.

In 1636 Key decided to move back to England, and he made arrangements for Elizabeth's godfather Humphrey Higginson to be her guardian for nine years. He stipulated that Higginson should treat Elizabeth like a family member and grant her freedom at fifteen. But Higginson did not keep his commitment to Elizabeth after elder Key died later that year. Instead, Higginson sold Elizabeth to Colonel

John Mottram, for whom she was required to serve the balance of her nine-year term before being released from bondage. Mottram took her to Northumberland County, and while there, she had a son with a young white lawyer named William Grinstead, an indentured servant himself.

After Mottram died in 1655, Elizabeth sued for her freedom after her late master's estate executors classified her and her infant son as "negroes" and part of the estate's property assets. She was unwilling to accept permanent servitude, so Elizabeth petitioned the colonial court for her freedom, as she had already served as an indentured servant for nineteen years.

Elizabeth claimed she was free-born under English common law as the father's position defined children's status. Elizabeth argued that as her white father was free-born, she could not be born into slavery. England's common law tradition of *partus sequitur patrem* was unambiguous, and Elizabeth was granted freedom, along with her son.

Reacting to the Key case... Virginia's House of Burgesses enacted a slave statute in 1661 without securing the King's permission, and then in 1662 purported to pass the hereditary slave statute of *partus sequitur ventrem* that could impose lifetime bondage on people based upon the legal status of the mother. The statute provided:

> "WHEREAS some doubts have arisen whether children got by any Englishman upon a negro woman should be slave or free. Be it, therefore, enacted and declared by this present grand assembly that all children borne in this country shall be bond or free according to the condition of the mother."

Virginia's hereditary slave statute decreed children of enslaved black females would be born into slavery, regardless of their father's race or status. However, this colonial statute was "repugnant" to English law, as it sought to change England's common law tradition of *partus sequitur patrem*... a patrilineal descent system to matrilineal. Soon, this scheme of hereditary slavery was emulated by nearly all other colonial assemblies within the British North American colonies. Slavery in colonial America was highly profitable, and it became endemic.

Then the legislative assembly amended the statute, condemning mixed-race children of free white women to serve as indentured servants for thirty years and subjecting the white mother to a fifteen-pound sterling fine. As punishment for having a mixed-race child... the white mother would be indentured for five years if she failed to pay the criminal fine within a month of the birth.

Targeted at black and mixed-race colonial-born children and women, Virginia's statutes and laws constituted the foundation of racial and gender discrimination in America. But these slave statutes, laws, and practices were extralegal as Virginia's legislative assembly never secured the King's permission. They violated English law and Virginia's colonial charter.

The extralegal practice of colonial slavery had been operating for over 100-years when King George III began his reign in 1761. Moreover, before the beginning of his power... the prior King's ministers replaced England's unofficial policy of salutary neglect with a new system, imperial administration. In furtherance, the *Declaratory Act of 1766* recalibrated the ascribed legislative role of colonial legislative assemblies within the North American colonies by legislatively abolishing "repugnant" colonial statutes, laws, votes, orders, resolutions, and related regulations... that rendered colonial slave statutes and racialized proceedings "utterly null and void to all intent and purposes whatsoever."

Parliament's *Declaratory Act of 1766* abolished colonial slave statutes, laws, orders, votes, proceedings, related racialized resolutions, and regulations. The practice of slavery was extralegal, and everything was returned to status *quo ante* in 1766 under English law.

Colonial slave statutes became void *ab initio* because they were "repugnant" to English law, violated the colonial charter, or purported to be lawful without the King's permission. All 13 legislative assemblies were affected. Its legislative members were disabused of the belief that they could enact colonial statutes, laws, votes, resolutions, and race-related regulations without first securing Parliament's permission or the King's consent.

The *Declaratory Act of 1766*, the British imperial government's renewed vigilance and appointment of new colonial governors, confirmed the end of England's unofficial policy of salutary neglect. Without a doubt, during this earlier period... the colonial government had abdicated colonial governance to its slaveholding colonial elite.

Immediately, colonial legislative assemblies became stymied and frustrated by the colonial charter. They were now required to abide by English law... which they were not doing... and needed to secure the King's permission unto any colonial statute or law. The legislative assemblies had never sought the King's permission before enacting a statute, and now they were required to do so, in furtherance of faithfully discharging the duties of their office in accordance to the English rule of law and each colonial charter.

Colonial slaveholding elites were engaged in a criminal conspiracy with colonial government officials. Colonial government officials were paid to refrain from vetoing colonial slave statutes that violated colonial charters and English law. The conspirators profited from purporting to enact colonial slave statutes and racialized rules, laws, and related regulations that exploited black colonists and Africans. They knew that they were criminally violating laws and oaths of high office. This extralegal practice of colonial slavery continued uninterrupted despite the legislative nullification of colonial slave statutes and now... possible criminal prosecutions and penalties. Further, it is telling that colonial government officials and slaveholding colonists did not complain about the *Declaratory Act of 1766*.

The colonials enumerated grievances in the Declaration serve as decisive proof that the leadership in colonial America knew the *Declaratory Act of 1766* had legislatively nullified colonial statutes, laws, resolutions, orders, and related regulations. Colonial statutes and laws were "repugnant" to established English law as they were enacted without securing the permission of England's monarch. All colonial charters required colonial assemblies to secure the monarchy's approval in furtherance of enacting a colonial statute or law. England's monarchy and its predecessors, Parliament under the *English Bill of Rights of 1689*, had to consent to enacted colonial statutes or laws once parliamentary sovereignty was declared.

Colonial legislative bodies, in passing colonial slave statutes and laws and related racialized regulations, had attempted to suspend (overrule) English laws, particularly *jus soli, partus sequitur patrem,* and the due process protections of English law, specified in England's *Magna Carta, Habeas Corpus Act of 1679* and the *English Bill of Rights of 1689*. The colonial legislative assemblies did not have plenary power to enact a statute without first securing the King's permission, nor did colonial assemblies have the authority to overrule or change existing English statutes and laws.

The *Declaratory Act of 1766* recalibrated the lawmaking authority of the colonial legislatures, reaffirmed Parliament's supreme power and colonial America's subordination to the laws of Great Britain as provided for in each colonial charter. Thus, all enacted colonial statutes and laws that challenged English law were legislatively nullified under the *Declaratory Act of 1766*. Under English law, the *Declaratory Act of 1766* returned black colonists suffering as slaves to status *quo ante*: the state of affairs existing *before* colonial assemblies purported to exercise plenary legislative powers and authority in derogation of colonial charters and English laws.

In a run-up to the American Revolution after Parliament enacted the *Declaratory Act* in 1766... all vestiges of colonial slavery, white privilege, and race-based regulations enacted by colonial legislatures within the American colonies were abolished. The ruling-class regulations defining and establishing the white race were repealed by the British imperial government in 1766. Black colonists were equal to white colonists under English law, and this had been the case for a decade when the Continental Congress adopted the Declaration of Independence. Black colonials who suffered as slaves to America's founding generation were lawfully liberated from slavery and it was quite significant that slaveholding colonials did not protest the *Declaratory Act of 1766*.

The news that Parliament passed the *Declaratory Act of 1766*, coupled with the repeal of the *Stamp Act* caused rejoicing up and down the seaboard. The colonial celebrations were marked by speeches, festive galas, and even the dedication and then erection of King George III's statue in New York City. In hindsight, the reception for the *Declaratory Act of 1766* was surprising since the Act had sweeping consequences upon colonial governance. Yet... few colonists voiced concerns or raised alarms to Parliament's use of its supreme powers and authority, by legislatively nullifying colonial statutes and racialized regulations or even its explicit declaration that Parliament had "full power and authority to make laws and statutes of sufficient force and validity to bind the colonies and people of America, subjects of the crown of Great Britain, in all cases whatsoever."

The *Declaratory Act* rendered colonial slave statutes and related racialized regulations void *ab initio*. Under English law... blacks born in colonial America suffering as slaves had their English subjecthood restored, and kidnapped Africans became indentured servants with a terminable period of servitude. The *Declaratory Act of 1766* abolished colonial slave statutes by English law.

The *Declaratory Act of 1766* plain meaning was that British colonists in North America were the Crown subjects who could be ruled over at

Parliament's pleasure. They had no say in their internal affairs. The *Declaratory Act of 1766* remained on England's law books until 1964, and for colonial governance, it was in alignment with English common law and all colonial charters. Parliament declared "all resolutions, votes, orders, and proceedings" in the colonies that denied or questioned Parliament's power and authority to make laws binding the colonies "in all cases whatsoever" were "utterly null and void" and rescinded the lawmaking authority granted to colonial legislative assemblies. This act abolished colonial slave statutes and racialized regulations ten years *before* the Declaration.

The *Declaratory Act of 1766* did not cause the colonists to protest its enactment. Most saw the Act as a mere restatement of the known and accepted constitutional state of colonial affairs. Moreover, colonial leadership saw a direct parallel to the *Dependency of Ireland on Great Britain Act of 1719*, also called the *Irish Declaratory Act of 1720*, which also stated Parliament had complete "authority to make laws and statutes of sufficient validity to bind the Kingdom and people of Ireland." Further, in 1766 lawyer and slaveowner John Randolph of the colony of Virginia, whose father was Sir John Randolph... the only Virginian to be knighted, stated that the *Declaratory Act* merely made explicit the constitutional state of colonial affairs established in 1689.

The *Declaratory Act of 1766* rendered all colonial statutes and laws null and void and rescinded and removed all colonial lawmaking power and authority from colonial legislative assemblies within North America. The colonies and their state of affairs were returned to status *quo ante* (pre-colonial legislature). By legislatively abolishing colonial statutes and laws, English law controlled as observed by jurist Blackstone in the classic treatise... "if an uninhabited or infidel territory was colonized by Britain, then English law automatically applied in this territory from the moment of colonization."

Doubtlessly, with the avoidance of colonial statutes and laws, all colonial slave statutes and laws became null and void in 1766. Colonial slavery became criminal, yet slavery within the North American colonies continued as Britain refused to subject colonial slaveholders to the rule of law. Thus, there was no outcry over the *Declaratory Act of 1766* until sporadic northern colonial rebellion erupted during the 1770s. Then in 1772... after the Twelve Judges of the Court of the King's Bench in the *James Somerset v. Charles Stewart* case ruled slavery was not "allowed and approved by the laws of this Kingdom," patriots like Patrick Henry, Thomas Jefferson, and John and Samuel Adams began invoking the Act as a symbol of parliamentary tyranny.

Firstly, Parliament's *English Bill of Rights of 1689* declared Parliament's supreme power over the colonies: parliamentary sovereignty. For generations, American legislatures accepted the supremacy of Parliament, and English courts affirmed it. Then, with King George III's approval, Parliament enacted the *Declaratory Act* declaring Parliament with "full power to make laws and statutes of sufficient force and validity to bind the colonies and people of America... in all cases whatsoever."

The *Declaratory Act* affirmed parliamentary sovereignty, legislatively abolished colonial statutes, laws, resolutions, votes, orders, proceedings, and reestablished the English rule of law in 1766. The Act sought to disabuse colonial legislative bodies of the idea that American legislature held power to enact statutes, laws, resolutions, votes, orders, and proceedings without Parliament's permission, and declared "all resolutions, votes, orders, and proceedings" in the colonies that denied or questioned Parliament's power and authority to make laws binding the colonies "in all cases whatsoever" were "utterly null and void to all in purposes whatsoever."

Furthermore, American legislatures enacted colonial slave statutes and passed resolutions that violated English law. Colonial legislative bodies, by enacting colonial slave statutes and related regulations "suspended" (overruled) English laws like *jus soli, partus sequitur patrem,* and the due process of English law, specified in England's *Magna Carta,* the *Habeas Corpus Act of 1679,* and the *English Bill of Rights of 1689* and did not seek or receive Parliament's consent. The colonial legislative assemblies did not have plenary power and authority to overrule or change English laws.

Thomas Jefferson later lamented that "by one Act they (Parliament) have suspended powers of American legislature and by another have declared they may legislate for us themselves in all cases whatsoever. These two acts alone form a basis broad enough whereon to erect a despotism of unlimited extent." But Parliament's *Declaratory Act* declaring parliamentary supremacy over colonial legislatures and suspending the devolved powers granted unto "American legislature" in 1766 was not an infringement upon colonial rights. The British Parliament had parliamentary sovereignty and the American legislatures never possessed plenary power to enact colonial slave statutes, laws, resolutions, votes, orders, or racialized regulations, as the legislative structure was bicameral. The putative colonial proceedings that enacted statutes, laws, resolutions, votes, orders, and racialized regulations were fatally defective since they failed to secure the King's permission.

Colonial assemblies took advantage of the turmoil created during the *English Civil Wars* during the early 1640s and bypassed securing the King's permission on colonial statutes and laws. Colonial statutes and laws enacted without the King's permission were legal nullities and laws, and such colonial statutes and laws, violated the *Sedition Act of 1661*... which made such actions by portended British lawmakers a treasonous offense. Further, Parliament was vested with the lawful power and authority to enact laws and repeal any law within the Kingdom... for a good reason or for no good reason.

The Parliamentarians won the *English Civil Wars*, and ultimately England's monarch consented to parliamentary sovereignty. The British monarch could not rule without the consent of Parliament, evidenced by the *English Bill of Rights of 1689, after* the institutional changes permitted by the *Glorious Revolution*. Further, the

English Bill of Rights of 1689 reaffirmed some rights guaranteed to subjects dated back to the *Magna Carta* and reflected in John Locke's influence on the document. Parliament conferred "basic rights" upon everyone living in colonial North America. This declaration included a strong statement that later became part of the American Constitution's First Amendment... "[T]hat it is the right of the subjects to petition the king, and all commitments and prosecutions for such petitioning are illegal." Further, Parliament's bill foreclosed excessive fines and cruel and unusual punishment... two essential concepts in the U. S. Constitution's Eighth Amendment.

Colonial slave statutes and racialized laws questioned Parliament's supreme powers and plenary authority to legislate over the colonies "in all casas whatsoever." Centrally, colonial slave statutes conflicted with English law prohibition slavery on its soil and the declarant that the right to liberty could not be capriciously changed, lessened, or abolished by the government without due process of English law. The English rule of law recognizes no person or body as having a right to override or set aside the legislation of Parliament. Further, colonial slave statutes and racialized regulations violated England's *Magna Carta of 1215*, Parliament's

Habeas Corpus Act of 1679, and the *English Bill of Rights of 1689* that incorporated in law the conviction that although some people may inherit privileges, all people in the Kingdom have "basic rights" that could not be infringed upon.

Varied English constitutional scholars such as A. V. Dicey opined that Parliament had the right to make or unmake any law whatever. Moreover, Parliament possessed plenary power to enact any statute or law and in having supreme legislative power could pass a law for good reason or no reason. Further, Dicey and other English constitutional scholars concluded that there were three sources for parliamentary sovereignty: (1) sovereignty by an Act of Parliament itself; (2) the complex relationship between all parts of government and their historical development and (3) the English courts that enforced all Acts of Parliament without exception. The Parliament of Great Britain was conferred parliamentary sovereignty over the colonies in North America by all three.

Objectively, colonial proceedings that enacted slave statutes, laws, resolutions, votes, orders, and racialized regulations violated Parliament's *pre*-colonial *Magna Carta of 1215,* clause 39, and *Parliament's Habeas Corpus Act of 1679.* Further, colonial assemblies questioned Parliament's enactment of the 1350 Act that conferred subjecthood and privileges to colonials "**for those who are born in Parts beyond the Seas**," the *General Charter of Emancipation of 1381* that abolished slavery on British soil, the *Royal Assent by Commission Act of 1541* that required the King's permission to all statutes and laws and the *Sedition Act of 1661* criminalizing a legislature's imputation of having "a legislative power without the King." And perhaps, the severity of purporting to enact statutes and laws without the King's permission best explains colonial America's muted response to the *Declaratory Act* when they became aware of its enactment in the spring of 1766.

Colonial statutes and racialized regulations that enslaved people in colonial America violated the *Magna Carta of 1215*, colonial charters and were the product of corrupt colonial government. The 13 colonial assemblies did not bother to secure the King's permission *before* purporting to authorize colonial slavery or overturn English common law traditions of *habeas corpus, jus soli*: birthright subjecthood, and *partus sequitur patrem*: a patrilineal descent system. Colonial slavery was an extralegal practice, as colonial slave statutes and all related racialized laws, orders, regulations, and resolutions were the product of corrupt colonial officials, graft, and colonial tyranny.

Although unnecessary, the imperial government had a good reason to abolish colonial slave statutes by the *Declaratory Act of 1766*. The enactment of slave statutes that violated the *Magna Carta of 1215* and overturned the English law of *partus sequitur patrem* in favor of a colonial law of *partus sequitur ventrem* during the early 1660s exceeded the devolved power of colonial assemblies. Hereditary slavery violated English law by denying birthright liberty to black colonials and violated Parliament's *Habeas Corpus Act of 1679* and the *English Bill of Rights of 1689*. In particular, "due process rights" and "Liberties" could not be taken away, abolished, or interfered with by the government in the absence of the due process of English law.

Moreover, foreigners in the realm had the right to due process under the rule of English law. With little debate, the enactment of slave statutes and related racialized regulations by colonial legislative assemblies that facilitated the subsequent passage of hereditary slave statutes and laws denied and questioned: "the power and authority of the parliament of Great Britain, to make laws binding the colonies." Doubtlessly, by enacting colonial slave statutes without the King of the imperial government's permission, colonial legislative assemblies had assumed and exercised Parliament's power and authority.

The era of salutary neglect officially came to an end in 1763, when the new Prime Minister George Grenville came into office. By placing a standing army in the colonies to protect against France's continual aggression at the end of the *Seven Years War*, Grenville advocated for Parliament to enact laws requiring that the colonists pay for the increased number of British troops. He concluded that since the colonists benefited from this defense, they should help pay for the army's cost through a series of taxes imposed by Parliament.

Most notably, Grenville's proposal of new taxes included the *Stamp Act* in 1765. It stated that the Parliament's taxing authority was the same in America as in Great Britain. However, the colony of Massachusetts formed the *Sons of Liberty* in the summer of 1765 to oppose the act... claiming their rights as Englishmen to be taxed only by their consent through their representative assemblies, as had been the practice for a century and a half. Parliament repealed the Act and concurrently passed the *American Colonies Act 1766*, commonly referred to as the *Declaratory Act of 1766*.

The *Declaratory Act* asserted the right of Parliament to pass laws for the American colonies, "in all cases whatsoever." The act recalibrated the imperial government's relationship with the American colonial legislatures by nullifying repugnant colonial statutes, laws, resolutions, votes, orders, proceedings, and racialized regulations that denied or challenged "the power and authority of the parliament of Great Britain, to make laws and statutes," restored colonial legislative affairs to status *quo ante*. And although colonial slave statutes were never lawful, after 1766, colonial statutes were rendered legislatively void, and colonial slavery and racialized laws and regulations were patently afoul of the rule of law, as Parliament held supreme legislative power and authority over colonial governments.

Objectively, colonial slave statutes and racialized regulations "denied and questioned" Parliament's power and control over the American colonies. These colonial statutes and laws denied Africans due process under English law authorized by the *Magna Carta of 1215*. Likewise, hereditary slave statutes denied and questioned the 1350 Act that conferred subjecthood and privileges to colonials **"For those who are born in Parts beyond the Seas,"** the *General Charter of Emancipation of 1381* that abolished and prohibited slavery on British soil and Parliament's *Habeas Corpus Act of 1679*.

Further, colonial American-born people being Englishmen by English law received powerful reaffirmation during the early 1800s. The British imperial government sanctioned the impressment of more than 15,000 American citizens into the British Royal Navy as a run-up to the *War of 1812*. The British imperial government did not recognize a right for a colonial-born citizen who was a British subject by law to relinquish his citizenship and become a citizen of another country. Thus, the British imperial government considered colonial-born Americans... British citizens. Therefore, the same was valid for black colonials born in colonial America *before* ratifying the *Definitive Treaty of Peace of 1783, making* the United States of America an independent nation. This was the same position that General Guy Carleton took when he and General George Washington met in May 1783.

Lastly, colonial assemblies' failure to secure the King's permission on hereditary slave statutes during the 1660s and beyond were questioning the *Royal Assent by Commission Act of 1541* and colonial charters that required the King's permission upon all statutes and laws and the *English Bill of Rights of 1689* since this Act had codified "basic rights" of everyone within the Kingdom. And without the King's permission, all such proceedings directly conflicted with Parliament's supreme powers and authority. Moreover, the *Sedition Act of 1661* made it a treasonable offense to promulgate a putative statute or even suggest "a legislative power without the king."

"We have abolished the slave, but the master remains." Abolitionist Wendell Phillips (*circa* 1865 after Congress enacted the 13th Amendment)

Chapter 4
The Constitution Reimagined

America's Declaration of Independence, drafted by Thomas Jefferson, and adopted by the Continental Congress on July 4, 1776, marks this nation's attempt to separate itself from the Empire of Great Britain. It identified various "unalienable rights." However, when Jefferson wrote "all men are created equal" in the preamble to the Declaration... he was not referring to individual equality. Instead, he meant that the American colonists, which did not exclude black colonials... had the same legal rights as other Englishmen and among them was "liberty." Furthermore, the grievance section in the Declaration of Independence where it is condemnatory of King George III and the British imperial government: "For taking our Charters, abolishing our valuable Laws, and altering fundamentally the Forms of our Governments" ... "He has refused his Assent to Laws, the most wholesome and necessary for the public good...

have revelatory implications upon the framers of the U. S. Constitution thinking about the nation's founding pivots on whether slaveholding Americans owned black colonials, most of whom were born in colonial America.

Firstly, the framers of the Constitution were blithely implicated in establishing a slaveholders' republic" that could protect slavery. Secondly, the framers knew that they could not attain that end without violating the rule of law and embracing white supremacy dogma. Black colonials had the same legal rights as white colonials due to the *Declaratory Act of 1766* that vested ten years before the Declaration of Independence. Thirdly, the condemnatory language in the Declaration that King George III had abolished..." "valuable Laws" and altered "fundamentally their Forms of Government" proves that the greatest tragedy of American constitutional history was not the failure of the framers to eliminate slavery in 1787... instead it was the subsequent emergence of a proslavery constitution and the set of compromises made during the Constitutional Convention, at the expense of black colonials who were British citizens and entitled to liberty.

Parliament's *Declaratory Act of 1766* abolished colonial slave statutes and racialized laws. The then young but rapidly-rising Jefferson had lamented that the British imperial government "by one Act they have suspended powers of American legislature and by another have declared they may legislate for us themselves in all cases whatsoever. These two acts alone form a basis broad enough whereon to erect a despotism of unlimited extent." Jefferson... the author of the Declaration of Independence, and the other founding fathers were knowledgeable that the *Declaratory Act of 1766* had abolished colonial statutes, racialized regulations, and returned erstwhile black slaves to status *quo ante*. It was a lawful exercise of the British imperial government's supreme legislative power.

Thus, when Jefferson's lamentation about the *Declaratory Act of 1766* is coupled with the most important statement of American ideals... the idea of the equality of humankind... black colonials were included since the British imperial government abolished colonial statutes in *"***all cases whatsoever***"* in 1766 and six years later... England's Court of the King's Bench declared in the *Somerset* case; slavery was not "allowed and approved by the laws of this Kingdom" in 1772. Yet, the U. S. government excluded black colonials and refused to serve the fundamental needs of the black people it governed. The U. S. government sustained the meritless claims of former slave owners that black colonials were chattel property and therefore excluded from the equality of humankind provision in the Declaration of Independence.

Shortly after that, the *Articles of Confederation and Perpetual Union* was written... America's first constitution of the United States. Written in 1777 and ratified on March 1, 1781, the states remained sovereign and independent, with Congress serving as the last resort on appeal of disputes. Congress named the new nation... The United States of America and while it gave to the central government substantial responsibilities, including the "common defence, the security of their liberties and their mutual and general welfare," it denied to the government most of the powers necessary to carry out those responsibilities... including the power to tax and to regulate commerce among the independent states.

Further, the central government had no power and authority to enforce the *Treaty of Paris of 1783* and the *Definitive Treaty of Peace of 1783* with the British government. These issues and the fact that the government could not prevent the landing of convicts that the British government continued to export to its former colonies or to "set at liberty" the 500,000 black Englishmen held in bondage throughout the nation led to a group of "nationalists" politicians to propose that the Continental Congress in New York call a "general convention." Congress delayed until February 21, 1787, then reluctantly agreed but limited any change to the mere "revising" of the existing *Articles of Confederation*.

James Madison of Virginia had different ideas for the general convention. He and other delegates had meetings before the Convention formally began its business on May 25, 1787. They concocted a plan to "amend" the Articles of Confederation and set the Convention's proceedings on a far more ambitious course. Together these men forged a radical new plan... the *Virginia Plan*, which shaped the course of events in 1787.

General George Washington had been the first to claim black colonials were lawfully owned by white Americans based upon "colonial statutes." This was a pronouncement made to General Guy Carleton after the *Treaty of Paris of 1783* was signed. Washington's statement of ownership was false since the British imperial government repealed "colonial statutes" by enacting Parliament's *Declaratory Act of 1766*. Nonetheless, Washington's meritless claim of ownership of black colonials based upon colonial statutes became America's dominant cultural narrative, and it served as America's legal justification for enacting a proslavery Constitution.

History supports, British General Guy Carleton summarily rejected Washington's ownership of black colonials in May of 1783. The two commanders met *after* the U. S. signed a peace truce ending America's Revolutionary War. Further, liberty was a personal right during colonial times. Thus, even if white colonials' ownership had not been nullified by the *Declaratory Act of 1766*, the Americans were legally required to prove their claims of ownership of black colonials under *R. v. Stapylton* (K.B. 1771).

Washington's claim was baseless since colonial statutes were never lawfully promulgated under English law. Further, white colonials could not prove ownership of black colonials based upon "colonial statutes" as a matter of English law. Moreover, the British imperial government rendered colonial slave statutes null and void through the *Declaratory Act of 1766*. Lastly, the *Somerset* decision struck down colonial slave statutes by finding that slavery was not "allowed and approved by the laws of this Kingdom" and can only be lawful by "positive law" in 1772. The status called slave ceased, and black colonials were restored to status *quo ante* by English law. But the U. S. did not free black colonials, nor were they conferred due process of law and, in violation of the *Definitive Treaty of Peace of 1783*, enslaved 500,000 black colonials based upon "colonial statutes" and require Americans to prove legal ownership of these people, although required by law. The wrongfully enslaved British citizens became the bedrock of America's slave-based economy. America's constitution went quite far to promote slavery and protect their baseless claims of ownership of British citizens.

During colonial times, by Parliament's *Royal Assent by Commission Act of 1541*, all statutes in the kingdom to have the force of law needed the King's permission. This principle was inflexible in that it was provided for in every colonial charter that all legislative proceedings in the colony were bicameral. Under pain of criminal law, Parliament's *Sedition Act of 1661* made it a treasonable offense for a legislature to even suggest "a legislative power without the King."

English law held that if a colonial statute did not have the King's permission, it was a legal nullity, and no one was obligated to adhere to it. Further, once a colonial statute is promulgated by a colonial assembly... the King is allowed to satisfy himself of its precise legal meaning and purpose and decide, and not before, whether he will grant his permission to it. If the King does not give his permission, his reason is supposed to be that he does not choose to make this colonial statute the law of the land. The fact that the colonial assembly has passed a statute for the King's consent or hope that he gives his permission means nothing by English law. The grievance section of the Declaration of Independence supports this position.

The *Declaratory Act of 1766* abolished slavery in colonial America and returned black colonials to status *quo ante*. However, the British imperial government's formalized repeal of colonial slave statutes and racialized laws only changed the rules of play, not the game of white domination itself, as white colonials continued enslaving blacks born in colonial America. Further, when the Declaration of Independence was adopted on July 4th in 1776... black colonials were not and could not be slaves under the English rule of law. Moreover, as colonial slavery ceased to exist by statute... black colonials were entitled to liberty and full citizenship as English citizens once the United States entered the *Definitive Treaty of Peace of 1783* that ended the Revolutionary War. However, 500,000 legally free black colonials became the bedrock of America's slave-based economy in derogating the rule of law, reinforced by a proslavery constitution.

Moreover, there is only one reason for constitutional law professors who are training America's future lawyers to ignore or reject the views of most historians, supported by evidence is that it would do inestimable damage to constitutionalism. The U. S. Constitution is not taught as a proslavery document that protected slavery and promoted slave ownership in America's law schools with rare exceptions. This is an anti-intellectual and disconcerting practice within America's law schools as just two generations ago, President John F. Kennedy observed that "the great enemy of truth is very often not the lie, deliberate, contrived, and dishonest... but the myth; persistent, persuasive, and unrealistic; too often we hold to the cliches of our forebears... we enjoy the comfort of opinion without the discomfort of thought." Further, Rev. Dr. Martin Luther King Jr. observed in his historic "*I Have a Dream*" speech in 1964... that "no lie can live forever,"... "truth crushed to the earth will rise again"... "Truth forever on the scaffold, wrong forever on the throne"... and "the Bible is Right. You shall reap what you sow."

Doubtlessly, critical race theory was not a deliberate countermeasure to the failure of constitutional law professors to teach the constitution as a proslavery document. Instead, Professor Derrick Bell led and developed new courses that studied law through a racial lens. Soon, Bell resigned from Harvard University because of what he viewed as the university's discriminatory practices. Then, in the early 1980s... student of color activists at Harvard Law School pushed the administration to hire a faculty of color to teach the new courses in Bell's absence. The university rejected students' requests, responding that no sufficiently qualified black instructor existed, and a white instructor was hired. The students organized protests and developed an "Alternative Course" using Bell's *Race, Racism, and American Law* (1973, 1st edition) as a core text.

The Alternative Course taught at Harvard University sought to understand why civil rights-era victories had stalled and eroded. The cohort examined and looked to the law to answer foundational questions surrounding enlightenment rationalism, legal equality, and constitutional neutrality and challenged the incrementalism approach of traditional civil-rights discourse. Critical race theorists date back to Frederick Douglass. They question as to whether and if the law could be used to dismantle race, racism, and racial inequity?

One hundred and sixty-nine years ago, the Ladies Anti-Slavery Society of Rochester invited Abolitionist Frederick Douglass to give a July Fourth speech. Douglass chose to speak on July 5, 1852... instead. He addressed an audience of about 600 in Corinthian Hall and delivered the historic speech... *What To A Slave Is the Fourth of July?* Douglass, a former slave, explored racial injustice and the broken promises of equality and liberty announced in the Declaration of Independence. It was a scathing speech in which Douglass stated: "This Fourth of July is yours, not mine; You may rejoice, I must mourn."

Douglass praised the founding generation, and he stated that the values expressed in the Declaration of Independence were "saving principles" and the "ringbolt of your nation's destiny," stating, "stand by those principles, be true to them on all occasions, in all places, against all foes, and at whatever cost." However, he asserted that slaves toiling in America owed nothing to and had no positive feelings towards the founders that insinuated slavery in America during colonial times. Douglass blasted these politicians who founded this nation for utter hypocrisy and betrayal of America's core values by establishing slavery in the United States.

"What have I, or those I represent, to do with your national independence? Are the great principles of political freedom and of natural justice embodied in that Declaration of Independence extended to us?... That, to the American slave, is your 4th of July? I answer; a day that reveals to him, more than all other days in the year, the gross injustice and cruelty to which he is the constant victim."

Essentially, Douglass's Fourth of July speech criticized his audience's boundless pride for a nation that claimed to value freedom and acclaimed allegiance to the rule of law. Yet, the founders created a regime of slavery in the United States and ignored the rule of law. Douglass found the claim that slavery was inherited from British rule to be feckless and disingenuous when juxtaposed to the notion that America was built upon the idea of liberty, freedom, and the rule of law... not men. Still, Douglass tells his audience that more than anything, it is built on uncontested claims, legal inconsistencies, and hypocrisies that have been overlooked for so long they appear to be truths.

Indeed, the threshold claims that colonial slavery was a legal institution during colonial times and black colonials were owned by Americans based upon "colonial statutes" are part of America's dominant cultural narrative. For these things to be true... colonial statutes and racialized regulations that conferred privileges unto white colonials had to be legal and unaffected by Parliament's legislative abolishment of repugnant colonial statutes and laws and were somehow totally exempt from becoming "utterly null and void to all in purposes whatsoever" by the *Declaratory Act of 1766*. Yet... there is no legal basis to support the suggestion that colonial statutes were ever lawfully promulgated during colonial times, nor did colonial statutes and racialized laws become exempt from the legal consequence imposed by Parliament's *Declaratory Act of 1766*. This exposes Washington's claim that colonial Englishmen owned colonial blacks to be untruthful and unlawful.

The main legal inconsistencies with Washington's claim that "colonial statutes" made black colonials the property of white patriots is that colonial slavery was an extralegal institution, and colonial statutes were never lawfully promulgated. And even if colonial slave statutes were legally promulgated, the *Declaratory Act of 1766* had legislatively abolished colonial statutes when the Declaration of Independence was adopted on July 4, 1776. Further, if colonial statutes were not abolished by Parliament's

Declaratory Act of 1766... then why in the Declaration itself... did the founding generation explicitly excoriate King George III for "abolishing our most valuable Laws?"

Second, the Continental Congress formally adopted English law in July 1776. Yet, they refused to honor the English rule of law by failing to require its American citizens to prove their ownership claim by the preponderance of evidence and to accord due process hearings for the 500,000 Revolutionary War-era blacks who were presumptively British citizens once America's legislature ratified the *Definitive Treaty of Peace of 1783* on January 14, 1784.

Douglass found the main hypocrisies were that the founding generation had rejected tyranny and second-class Englishmen treatment for themselves, declaring King George III was a tyrant. Yet, they were perfectly fine with creating a new nation that enslaved and exploited black people in total violation of the established rule of law. History supports, white colonials enslaved 500,000 black colonials in violation of the English rule of law post-ratification of the *Definitive Treaty of Peace of 1783*.

Finally, Douglass makes the case that the United States is the object of mockery and often contempt among the various nations of the world for its claim of being an exceptional nation. History supports... "colonial statutes" were rendered null and void by the *Declaratory Act of 1766*. Further, during colonial times... England's high court declared slavery as a practice was not "allowed and approved by the laws of this Kingdom" and could only be lawful by "positive law" in 1772. Yet, America has brazenly justified the creation of a slave nation.

Doubtlessly, the Declaration of Independence was a product of grievance politics. The grievance was that the British imperial government abolished colonial slave statutes through the *Declaratory Act of 1766*, stripping colonial slavery of its pretextual lawfulness. Further, in June 1772... England's Court of the King's Bench affirmed parliamentary sovereignty in the *James Somerset v. Charles Stewart* habeas case that freed Somerset and proclaimed slavery was not "allowed and approved by the laws of this Kingdom." This judicial decision was controlling precedent in colonial America. The court decision returned black colonials to status *quo ante* and struck down colonial slave statutes and laws. The Court of the King's Bench reaffirmed that slavery within the Kingdom could only be a legal condition if enacted by a "positive law" passed by the British

Parliament... not one branch of a colonial legislature without the permission of England's King.

Parliament's exercise of its supreme legislative power, parliamentary sovereignty rendered colonial slave statutes and racialized regulations such as the hereditary law of *partus sequitur ventrem* "utterly null and void for all purposes for whatsoever" in 1766. By law, Parliament's *Declaratory Act of 1766* was a recalibration of the colonial government... that led to the recall of colonial governors, suspension of the colonial legislatures, and abolishing repugnant colonial legislative proceedings, including racialized resolutions, votes, and regulations. The legal consequence of Parliament's act restored black colonials' liberty rights, returned those suffering as slaves to status *quo ante,* and reinstated their complete protection of English law. The *Somerset* decision six years after Parliament's *Declaratory Act of 1766* was the death knell for colonial slavery in the British colonies in America, and white slaveholding colonials knew it.

In 1865, abolitionist Wendell Phillips, upon remarking about the enactment of the 13th Amendment, made the prescient comment that the U. S. Congress had "abolished the slave, but the master remains." Likewise, it was the same thing that the British imperial government did in

1766 when they failed to hold colonial officials and slaveholding colonials to account for their criminal behavior after abolishing colonial slave statutes and racialized laws and regulations.

History accounts, there was a major miscalculation on the part of the British imperial government. The colonial officials who enacted repugnant colonial statutes and laws that placed black colonials *below* the rule of English law during colonial times and colonial slave masters who exploited black colonials were not held to account for their criminal behavior. Decidedly, these British colonials were all criminals as they had conspired to create a criminal enterprise... no less misanthrope and depraved than the trafficking in children today.

Further, colonial slavemasters did not cease their unlawful activities even after Parliament destroyed their colonial safe harbor. Nonetheless, given the *Sedition Act 1661* that criminalized enacting statutes or laws without the King's permission and the reckless violations of the bi-cameral structure of the colonial legislature... colonial government officials were concerned. Thus, there were no organized protestations advanced by colonials in response to the *Declaratory Act of 1766*... and this was not blind luck.

Doubtlessly, colonial legislators who purported to enact colonial slave statutes and racialized regulations feared criminal prosecution and assured conviction in England for purporting to enact statutes and laws without the King's permission. Further, colonial slavemasters, their partners in crime, were fearful too. The fears of slaveholding colonials and their dissatisfaction with the British colonial officials they paid for protection grew. These two things were the underpinning of their grievances with the imperial government and King George III. These grievances festered, fermented, and stewed. Defending their family's freedom, wealth, and reputation was now at the top of the slaveholding colonials' list of priorities once the *Somerset* decision struck down colonial slave statutes in 1772.

Equal treatment under the rule of law was one of two core features of England's *Magna Carta*, signed by King John in 1215. Moreover, the second core feature was that everyone would be granted equal protection under English law and accorded due process. Among its many provisions, the *Magna Carta* declared that no person should be deprived of their liberty or property "except by the lawful judgement of his equals or by the law of the land." Belatedly, the

British imperial government recognized that in allowing a vast swart of people to do things against other people in violation of the rule of law, the colonial government had weakened the core principle that the law is king. Yet, the *Magna Carta* became the cornerstone of America's constitutionalism, but black colonials were enslaved without being accorded due process.

The Declaration of Independence offered erstwhile Englishmen who became Americans an opportunity to start anew and put in practice what they had experienced and learned from England's governance in the American colonies. However, the Continental Congress did not take advantage of this opportunity and assaulted the rule of law when they placed black colonials *below* the rule of law *after* ratifying the *Definitive Treaty of Peace* on January 14, 1784.

Revisionist historians and others will freely call reimagining the Declaration of Independence… critical race theory or say "so what," given the distance America has traveled as a nation since 1776. And with little debate… those who might say such things are opposing justice for the descendants of colonial slaves, truth-telling, and reconciliation. Yet, such utterances and positions are purposeful and reasoned. They foresee a historical reckoning and understand it as an existential threat to the dominant cultural narrative and U. S. constitutionalism. Further, teaching critical race theory to children will encourage intellectual curiosity and will help to refine their investigative and critical thinking skills.

Reimagining the Constitution is an opportunity to recalibrate America's historiography. Colonial statutes and racialized laws and regulations that conferred privileges unto white colonials were legal nullities due to a legislative act of the British imperial government in 1766. Thus, when the Continental Congress adopted the Declaration of Independence on July 4, 1776... all-black colonials were "free negroes." Validating the claim that 500,000 Revolutionary War-era blacks were unlawfully enslaved, and the Framers of America's constitution aided in the unlawful exploitation of free people by placing 11 clauses in the Constitution that legitimize slavery can create dissonance for many... but facts are incredibly stubborn and will persist.

Doubtlessly, these stubborn facts must be revealed and then acknowledged by America's government. Accepting and acknowledging these irrefutable facts are essential to this nation's future and its continued prominence on the world stage. Further, it is essential to the descendants of those black colonials suffering from intergenerational trauma. It is, as author James Baldwin observed, "to accept one's past; one history... is not the same thing as drowning in it; it is learning how to use it. An invented past can never be used. It cracks and crumbles under the pressures of life, like clay in a season of drought."

The *Declaratory Act* nullified all colonial slave statutes, laws, resolutions, votes, orders, and proceedings because they questioned Parliament's supreme legislative power and authority over the American colonies in 1766. Then the *Somerset* decision declared slavery was not "allowed and approved by the laws of this Kingdom" and struck down colonial slave statutes and laws in 1772. The condition called "slave" was a legal nullity when Thomas Jefferson penned the Declaration of Independence in 1776.

Historians have tried to explain Jefferson's preamble in the Declaration and commitment to the institution of human slavery as contradictory. They were not. Instead, Jefferson, a lawyer, slavemaster, and an efficient young man of 29 years... recognized that it was impossible to create a virtuous, sustainable democratic nation while enslaving blacks and, in acting upon that knowledge, wanted the Continental Congress to adopt Roman law as the nation's jurisprudence formally. However, Jefferson was disappointed when his Roman law bill was rejected, and they then formally adopted English law after adopting the Declaration on the Fourth of July 1776. This created a problem for Jefferson, a devotee of the British political theorist John Locke, who posited that the most precious thing man has is property and was anti-slavery. Locke defined property as Life, Liberty, and Estate.

Locke's terms... property encompassed material things and ownership of self, so slavery was neither justifiable nor contemplated by Locke in his *Two Treatises of Government*. Locke also took the position that slavery conflicted with natural law. Locke's perspectives concerning liberty and the social contract not only influenced Jefferson, but Locke's writings also influenced Alexander Hamilton, James Madison, and other founding Fathers of the United States.

Given his knowledge, Jefferson saw Roman law as the only possible way to blunt the legal consequence of the British imperial government's nullification of colonial statutes, laws, and racialized regulations that supported white supremacy. Then the Court of the King's Bench issued the *Somerset* decision that slavery was not "allowed and approved by the laws of this

Kingdom" in 1772. This *pre*-Declaration of Independence action of the British imperial government was the final nail in the coffin of the corrupt colonial governmental apparatus that had protected the criminal practice called slavery for nearly a century. Being so informed, by 1774... In addressing the Virginia assembly, Jefferson stated: "[T]he abolition of domestic slavery is the greatest object of desire in these colonies, where it was unhappily introduced in their infant state."

Jefferson's perspective was merely in line with the English rule of law. He was the first lawmaker in a colony dependent upon slave labor to discuss the chattel slavery issue in this manner.

The adoption of English law meant that black colonials were the countrymen of white colonials... not their property. Additionally, since Parliament's *Declaratory Act of 1766* had abolished colonial statutes which violated colonial charters... the Americans could never prove legal ownership of black colonials, as a matter of law. The U. S. enslaved 500,000 colonial blacks and, for generations, has portrayed slavery's insinuation here in America as a legal practice... authorized by colonial statutes and inherited from British rule. But in fact, slavery in America has a criminal origin that has been hidden by a myth.

Further, there is academic support for the proposition that "the Constitution is best understood... as a means of implementing the rights outlined in the Declaration." Stephen B. Presser, *Book Review*, 14 Const. Comment., 229 (1997).

Moreover, the actions of the Framers of the federal constitution were self-serving when you consider, as an observant student of the constitutional history observed that "[t]he Founders deliberately omitted the Declaration's doctrine of equal rights from the *Bill of Rights*, not because the doctrine was considered more rhetoric, but because its inclusion in the Constitution would have been dangerous to the continued existence of slavery." Robert J. Reinstein, *Completing the Constitution: The Declaration of Independence, Bill of Rights and Fourteenth Amendment*, 66 Temple L. Rev. 361, 362-363 (1993).

Most symbolic, James Madison... the Father of the Constitution and the fourth president of the United States, had a pivotal role in drafting and promoting the Constitution and the *Bill of Rights*. He owned one hundred black American colonists while writing, arguing, and officiating over the federal constitution. If he legally held them, that's one discussion, but it topples the constitutional process if he did not.

The Framers could not lawfully enter into any partisan compromises with slaveholding Americans by declaring colonial blacks were three-fifths of a person and or in any way disfranchise black colonials during the 1780s to hold the union together, although they did... but they did so extralegally. Thus, the Framers of the federal constitution inalterably sullen and compromised the U. S. constitutional process.

Singularly, the defeat of Jefferson's Roman law bill devastated the belated claim that black colonials who held the same legal status as white colonials under English law on July 4, 1776, were somehow excluded from the idea of equality under the law announced in the Declaration. Moreover, Jefferson wrote in 1823 that the Continental Congress "mangled" the Declaration since he had based his perspective and ideas upon Locke. After adopting the Declaration of Independence... the *Declaratory Act of 1766*, and the *Somerset* decision controlled by binding themselves to the English rule of law.

The Continental Congress adopted the ideal in the Declaration that all colonials were equal to Englishmen under the rule of law. This perspective is plain since one passage from John Locke's *Second Treatise* was restated verbatim in the Declaration, referencing a "long train of abuses." Jefferson based the Declaration on Locke's views that rejected slavery, and such was Locke's influence upon Jefferson that he even wrote:

> "Bacon, Locke, and Newton... I consider them as the three greatest men that have ever lived, without exception, and as having laid the foundation of those superstructures which have been raised in the Physical and Moral sciences."

Abraham Lincoln reimagined the Declaration of Independence in 1857. Lincoln rejected the view advanced by politicians of the day that the Constitution was a justification for slavery. In this respect, Lincoln's views converged with Douglass, and it was on full display in his June 1857 speech on the *Dred Scott* case, a legal case involving the thorny question of whether slavery would be permitted in new territories.

Over the decades, many compromises had been made to avoid disunion. But what did the Constitution say on this question? This issue was raised in 1857 *before* the United States Supreme Court in *Dred Scott v. Sandford*.

Dred Scott was a slave of an army officer, John Emerson. Scott had been taken from Missouri to Illinois and Minnesota for several years in the

1830s before returning to Missouri. The *Missouri Compromise of 1820* had declared the area, including Minnesota, free. In 1846, Scott sued for his freedom because he had lived in a free state and a free territory for a prolonged period of time.

Finally, after eleven years, Scott's case reached the Supreme Court and in a (7-2) ruling found that a slave (Dred Scott) who had resided in a free state and territory (where slavery was prohibited) was not thereby entitled to his freedom; that African Americans were not and could not be citizens of the United States; and that the *Missouri Compromise* (1820), which had declared free all territories west of Missouri and north of latitude 36°30', was unconstitutional.

The *Dred Scott* decision added fuel to the sectional controversy and pushed the country closer to civil war. Further, in June 1857, Republican Abraham Lincoln responded to a speech delivered two weeks earlier by Democrat Stephen Douglas in which Douglas had applauded the Supreme Court's decision on the *Dred Scott* case that answered the question: "Can a negro, whose ancestors were imported into this country, and sold as slaves, become a member of the political community formed and brought into existence by the Constitution of the United States, and as such become entitled to all the rights, and privileges, and immunities, guarantied by that instrument to the citizen? One of which rights is the privilege of suing in a court of the United States in the cases specified in the Constitution."

Lincoln rejected the finding of the Supreme Court that "the legislation and histories of the times, and the language used in the Declaration of Independence, show, that neither the class of persons who had been imported as slaves, nor their descendants, whether they had become free or not, were then acknowledged as a part of the people, nor intended to be included in the general words used in that memorable instrument."

Further, the court found that "[T]hey had for more than a century before been regarded as beings of an inferior order, and altogether unfit to associate with the white race, either in social or political relations; and so far inferior, that they had no rights which the white man was bound to respect; and that the negro might justly and lawfully be reduced to slavery for his benefit."

Lincoln, who lived in Illinois, disagreed with the U. S. Supreme Court's decision, as did most Northerners who felt that the next step would be for the Supreme Court to decide that no state could exclude slavery under the Constitution, regardless of their wishes or laws. And in his speech, Lincoln detailed the hardships

Americans endured when they were British colonies and validated their collective feelings of ill-treatment. Then like Douglass's Fourth of July speech five years earlier, Lincoln highlighted the irony of their inability to sympathize with black people they oppressed in cruel ways that the forefathers they valorized never experienced.

Further, Lincoln explained that the Declaration of Independence was "meant to set up a standard maxim for a free society, which should be familiar to all, and revered by all; constantly looked to, constantly labored for, and even though never perfectly attained, constantly approximated." Lincoln added, "the assertion that 'all men are created equal' was of no practical use in effecting our separation from Great Britain, and it was placed in the Declaration, nor for that, but for "future use." Singularly, the Fourth of July allows us all to "constantly" approximate this standard maxim of a free society called America.

Nonetheless, it is a fair characterization to say… Lincoln did not wage a holy war to free black slaves, nor did he believe in equal civil rights for blacks. And Frederick Douglass did not doubt Lincoln's position on the question, given how often he repeated them. One need only consider Lincoln's remarks during one of his celebrated debates with Stephen Douglas in 1858, as they competed for an Illinois Senate seat.

"I will say then that I am not, nor ever have been in favor of bringing about in any way the social and political equality of the white and black races... that I am not nor ever have been in favor of making voters or jurors of negroes, nor of qualifying them to hold office, nor to intermarry with white people, and I will say in addition to this that there is a physical difference between the white and black races which I believe will forever forbid the two races living together on terms of social and political equality."

Moreover, Lincoln never publicly denounced these views. Still, his campaign for the presidency two years later saw Douglass and other abolitionists supporting his candidacy... which he won, and soon a devastating civil war followed.

After the South started the Civil War, Lincoln stated that his primary purpose in waging war was to save the Union... not to end slavery. One of his most straightforward responses was to Horace Greeley, editor of the *New York Tribune*, who had criticized Lincoln for failing to make the Civil War a war for abolition. Lincoln replied, in part:

"My paramount object in this struggle is to save the Union, and it is not either to save or to destroy slavery. If I could save the Union without freeing any slave, I would do it; and if I could save it by freeing all the slaves, I would do it; and if I could save it by freeing some and leaving others alone, I would also do that. What I do about slavery and the colored race, I do because I believe it helps to save the Union; and what I forbear, I forbear because I do not believe it would help to save the Union."

Consistent with this position, Lincoln's *Emancipation Proclamation* was explicitly proffered as a "war measure." On varied occasions, Lincoln explained his reasons for issuing the Proclamation. For example, the day after the preliminary *Proclamation* was issued, September 13, 1862, when he met with a delegation of abolitionist Christian ministers and told them plainly:

"Understand, I raise no objections against it [slavery] on legal or constitutional grounds... I view the matter [emancipation] as a practical war measure, to be decided upon according to the advantages or disadvantages it may offer to the suppression of the rebellion."

In furtherance, Lincoln's *Emancipation Proclamation* proclaimed freedom only in those areas that were under Confederate control, and the proclamation promised that those states that returned to the Union within 100 days could keep their slaves. The four slave states in the Union... the so-called Border States, were unaffected by the Proclamation. As one contemporary critic remarked, Lincoln's *Emancipation* applied only to those slaves that Lincoln could not help.

Lincoln spoke at the dedication of the Gettysburg battlefield cemetery on November 19, 1863. In a relatively brief speech, Lincoln asserted that the nation was born not in 1789, but in 1776... "conceived in Liberty and dedicated to the proposition that all men are created equal." He defined the war as being dedicated to the principles of liberty and equality for all, announced in the Declaration of Independence. He pledged that the countless deaths would not be in vain, that slavery would end, and the future of democracy would be assured, that "government of the people, by the people, for the people, shall not perish from the earth." Defying Lincoln's prediction that "the world will little note, nor long remember what we say here," the *Gettysburg Address* became, arguably, the most quoted speech in American history.

"As soon as a Negro comes to England... he is free; one may be a villien in England... but not a slave." Lord Chief Justice John Holt (circa 1702)

Chapter 5
Annualized Reckoning

Fourth of July is an annualized holiday for reckoning America's core idea of equality of citizenship. Parliament's *Declaratory Act of 1766* legislatively abolished colonial slave statutes and racialized laws and regulations authorizing hereditary slavery of colonial-born blacks... ten years *before* the Declaration of Independence was adopted. People born in colonial America were Englishmen by birth. Further, four years after the *Declaratory Act* was passed... England's King's Bench struck down colonial slave statutes in the *Somerset* decision in 1772.

Yet, while most Americans might see the Fourth as a day to celebrate, a descendant of a colonial American slave or Juneteenth blacks should know the day as a time to rededicate themselves to push thought-leaders, politicians, and government officials to honor the unfulfilled idea of individual equality under the rule of law, historical justice for their ancestors and to challenge the rampant, malignant philosophy of majoritarian politics and white supremacy this day in our multiethnic country.

Doubtlessly, the message of *"Make America Great Again"* and the siege of our nation's capital on January 6th is harkening back to an age of majoritarian politics when white people controlled everything on behalf of white people and when everyone else was accorded second-class citizenship. However, as the British imperial government abolished the racialized colonial regulation called *partus sequitur ventrem* in 1766, all colonial-born blacks were Englishmen by birth. Thus, America was multiethnic, not a white nation when it was created in 1776. Further, people of African ancestry fought for independence alongside white colonials, and of course, Native Americans were here when the British arrived in the late 16th century.

Further, tiered citizenship violated English law and is antithetical to the Declaration of Independence's core idea of equality under the rule of law, and what each 4th of July should mean to a descendant of an American slave is a day of assessment, reflection, and solemnity, and ever so needed presently here in this country as Mukul Kesavan in *The New York Review of Books* states that "majoritarian politics results from the patiently constructed self-image of an aggrieved, besieged majority that believes itself to be long-suffering and refuses to suffer in silence anymore." Moreover, the manifestation and cultivation of this injury can be actual, contrived, or imaginary and lead to rebellions, lynchings, and ethnic cleansing.

As opposed to a constitutional democracy, majoritarian refers to a democracy based upon the majority rule of a society's citizens. They fear losing their remaining privileges, like police officer Derek Chauvin's entitlement to bring any black man to heel and not being subject to any personal accountability for criminal behavior or violating George Floyd's civil rights. This is challenging times, as conservatives attack the teaching of critical race theory, the callous indifference of politicians in Washington to respond to domestic threats or to authorize an investigation to protect the nation from foreign threats when coupled with the ongoing actions of state legislatures throughout the country to restrict the right to vote of non-white Americans supports. Thus, this experiment in a democracy called America is in peril.

And looking back at early colonial times, one must be struck by what can only be called equality of oppression. Virginia's colonial assembly and the British ruling class created majoritarianism based upon being "white" during the 1670s. Working together in the same fields, sharing the same huts, the same situation caused colonials to have the same grievances. And the laboring class living in colonial America showed little interest in having a racial identity before Virginia's ruling class created an institution of race-based privileges. This policy soon divided colonials based upon race, and over time, racialized attitudes and the ideology of white supremacy became integral. Before such time, everyone defined themselves ethnically.

Virginia's *Bacon Rebellion of 1676* was the impetus for this race-based policy initiative as this was an armed rebellion joined in by all classes of colonists. The alliance of European indentured servants, Afro-Englishmen, and Africans disturbed Virginia's colonial ruling class. They responded by hardening the racial caste of slavery to divide the two races from future united uprisings. Within European traditions, darker-skinned people were universally stigmatized as laborers and servants, as it was a characteristic of most who worked outside in the sun and elements. This contributed to its effectiveness and acceptance as it was based upon European values and caste traditions.

Over time, Virginia's policy of white-skinned privilege became a dominant cultural narrative. This policy was furthered by corruption, political graft, and racialized terrorism. White colonials came to see unearned privileges as an entitlement and a license to discriminate, terrorize, and take advantage of all non-white people within the colony.

Virginia's policy of white-skinned privilege came to define and shape the social, political, legal, and labor systems of colonial America. But then, the British imperial government passed Parliament's *Declaratory Act of 1766* that rendered this white-skinned policy, colonial slave statutes, and racialized regulations "utterly null and void." This abolishment of colonial slave statutes and racialized regulations happened ten years *before* the Declaration of Independence on July 4, 1776.

Thomas Jefferson lamented that the British imperial government "by one Act had suspended powers of American Legislature and by another have declared they may legislate for us themselves in all cases whatsoever. These two acts alone form a basis broad enough whereon to erect a despotism of unlimited extent."

While drafting the Declaration, Jefferson knew, as did every patriot when adopting the Declaration on the Fourth of July 1776, that Parliament had lawfully exercised its power and authority when it nullified colonial slave statutes, especially those that questioned Parliament's supreme authority or those enacted without the King's permission. Without the King's permission, all such proceedings directly conflicted with Parliament's *Royal Assent by Commission Act of 1541*. Moreover, the *Sedition Act of 1661* made it a treasonable offense to promulgate a putative statute or even suggest "a legislative power without the king." Thus, enacting a colonial statute or any law without the King's permission was a grave violation of the English rule of law.

The British imperial government's nullification of race-based colonial statutes, laws, orders, resolutions, proceedings and racialized regulations such as *partus sequitur ventrem* in 1766 caused a sea change in colonial America. Hereditary slavery ceased to be a legal practice in colonial America. The *Declaratory Act of 1766* not only rendered all colonial proceedings "utterly **null and void**," it returned black colonists suffering as colonial slaves to status *quo ante* and stunned the slaveholding colonists since it altered "**fundamentally the Forms of [colonial]**

our governments," as stated in the Declaration of Independence.

The colonial slavemasters were stripped of all putative economic value in these black colonials, and under no circumstance could they lawfully claim ownership over these people based upon colonial statute. Thus, the *Declaratory Act of 1766* wholly altered colonial governance and its society... and white colonials knew this to be the case. Further, adopting the Declaration of Independence on July 4, 1776, was the slaveholding patriots' plan to galvanize the relationship between themselves and non-slaveholding patriots. The plan worked, as the idea of individual equality of colonials captured by the Declaration's preamble was a pronouncement of English law.

Virginia's Governor Lord Dunmore's issued the British imperial government's *Southern Strategy Proclamation* in November 1775 that emancipated colonial slaves and recruited them to fight against the patriots. Patriot James Madison felt the British's Southern *Strategy Proclamation* was the kind of "tampering with the slaves" that he had most feared. "To say the truth," he confided in a friend... "that is the only part in which this colony is vulnerable, we shall fall like Achilles by the hand of one that knows that secret." But, in having been the slaveholding colonists partner-in-crime for nearly a century, the British imperial government knew the slaveholding patriots' "secret." And it was because of this shared secret... black colonists became a factor in the rebellion.

Worried, General George Washington, in his capacity as both commander-in-chief of the Continental Army and a concerned slaveholding patriot... felt that it was necessary to crush the British's slave recruitment campaign, or the momentum of slave defections and enlistments in the imperial army would be "like a snowball rolling down a hill." Governor Dunmore's proclamation caused Washington to believe, as he stated in a letter to Colonel Henry Lee III in December 1775, that success in the rebellion would come down to whatever side could arm "negroes" the fastest.

The Continental Congress is fully informed, and acting upon this knowledge, this legislature reversed Washington's prohibition of black enlistment in the Continental Army. As a result, although their risks in running away had never been more significant, enslaved blacks left captivity. This caused the U. S. legislature to promise freedom to its black recruits and placed them within the ambit of the Declaration of Independence. Becoming a free colonist was the legal consequence for blacks suffering as slaves in 1766 since there were no tiered subjects of King George III by English law. Absent being under an indentured contract with a defined period of servitude, all-black colonials, including people born in Africa, were free Englishmen under the English rule of law. They were countrymen of the slaveholding patriots by law, not their property.

The Continental Congress adopted the English rule of law *after* declaring independence of British rule. The English rule of law provided for no differentiation between black and white colonials in 1776. Black colonists had the same right to self-government and to assume a "separate and equal station" among other nations as white colonials. Further, just like other loyalists, black colonists were not compelled to leave the U. S. and could not be disfranchised of any legal rights. Moreover, citizenship through tacit consent was conferred unto all English citizens who continued to reside in the United States after the *Definitive Treaty of Peace* was ratified in 1784.

The conference of U. S. citizenship unto all colonial Englishmen regardless of race was underpinned by the "no slavery allowed" aspect of the British constitution, the *English Bill of Rights of 1689*, and English law that espoused the principle that citizenship "ought to be uniform, and without invidious gradations and it ought to confer equal rights."

The ratification of the peace treaty meant Revolutionary War-era blacks were British subjects, and according to the holding of the Court of the King's Bench in *R. v. Stapylton* in 1771... the Americans who claimed ownership of former black colonists had the legal burden of proving ownership of that person under "colonial statutes." Absent doing so, that former black colonist had full U. S. citizenship and was entitled to liberty, effective July 1776 under the rubric of tacit consent. The 500,000 Revolutionary War-era blacks were the slaveholding patriots George Washington, Thomas Jefferson, James Madison, John Marshall, and Patrick Henry's countrymen under the English American rule of law, not slaves.

In *The Atlantic* in 2014... journalist and writer Ta-Nehisi Coates wrote an essay titled *The Case for Reparations*. He challenged each and everyone to consider that "To celebrate freedom and democracy while forgetting America's origins in a slavery economy was patriotism a la carte"... "If Thomas Jefferson's genius matters, then so do his taking of Sally Hemings' body. If George

Washington crossing the Delaware matters, so must his ruthless pursuit of the runagate Oney Judge". The fidelity to which America's first and third presidents of the United States held towards the rule of law before and during their presidency must always matter.

Jefferson, a United States Envoy and Minister to France, brought a fourteen-year-old Sally Hemings to Paris in 1787. He fathered children with this young black girl... while Washington fixated on recapturing Oney Judge. Both young girls should have been "set at liberty" under the *Definitive Treaty of Peace of 1783* and protected by the rule of law. However, these legally free black English citizens born in colonial Virginia in 1773 before the Declaration of Independence were deemed Jefferson and Washington's slaves based on "colonial statutes" and the U. S. constitution.

Sally Hemings was born in Charles City County, Virginia, in 1773... seven years after the *Declaratory Act* abolished hereditary slave statutes and the year following the *Somerset* decision. This determination by the Court of the King's Bench especially struck down Virginia's colonial slave statutes. Hemings was the biological daughter of *white* Englishman John Wayles, Thomas Jefferson's father-in-law. Thus, according to the colonial court's holding in the Elizabeth Key case, she was an Englishman by birth as her white father was a free-born Englishman.

Parliament's *Declaratory Act of 1766* abolished all colonial slave statutes, including Virginia's 1662 hereditary slave law of *partus sequitur ventrem*. Moreover, the *Somerset* decision declared slavery was not "allowed and approved by the laws of this Kingdom" and rejected the legal sufficiency of Virginia's slave statutes and hereditary slave laws in 1772. Hemings was part of Martha Jefferson's inheritance from her father, John Wayles, and history supports Hemings came to Jefferson's Monticello home as an infant.

The facts are materially the same for Oney Judge, born in Mount Vernon, Virginia, in 1773. Judge was the biological daughter of *white* Englishman Andrew Judge, George Washington's tailor. Thus, according to the colonial court's holding in the Elizabeth Key case, she too was an Englishman by birth. The court sustained Key's legal contention that she could not be born into slavery as her white father was free-born. Further, the *Declaratory Act of 1766* abolished all colonial slave statutes and abolished Virginia's hereditary slave law of *partus sequitur ventrem* enacted in 1662. Moreover, the *Somerset* decision declared slavery was not "allowed and approved by the laws of this Kingdom" rejecting the legal sufficiency of Virginia's slave statutes and racialized laws in 1772.

On June 30, 1779... by way of the *Phillipsburg Proclamation*, the British General Henry Clinton freed all enslaved people living within the North American colonies, including Hemings and Judge's mothers and the then six-year-old colonial born girls whose fathers were *white* Englishmen. Significantly, Virginia's charter of 1606 provided in relevant part the following:

> "Also we do, for Us, our Heirs, and Successors, DECLARE, by these Presents, that all and every the Persons being our Subjects, which shall dwell and inhabit within every or any of the said several Colonies and Plantations, and every of their children, which shall happen to be born within any of the Limits and Precincts of the said several Colonies and Plantations, shall HAVE and enjoy all Liberties, Franchises, and Immunities, within any of our other Dominions, to all Intents and Purpose, as if they had been abiding and born, within this our Realm of England, or any other of our said Dominions."

Hemings and Judge were English citizens by birth under *partus sequitur patrem* and *jus soli*. Colonial-born black colonists such as Hemings and Judge, whose fathers were white Englishmen, were deemed "**children of the King,**" protected by Parliament's 1350 "**statute for those who are born in Parts beyond Sea.**" This Act protected Hemings and Judge's ancestral English common law birthrights since their fathers were white Englishmen.

The *Declaratory Act of 1766* specifically abolished all colonial proceedings that questioned Parliament's power or denied Parliament's authority to make binding laws in colonial America. The *Declaratory Act of 1766* made Virginia's hereditary slave statutes null and void and made free-born English citizens of Hemings and Judge in 1773, as a matter of English law. Further, Parliament's *1350 Act* for those born in Parts beyond the Seas, *the General Charter of Emancipation of 1381, and the Royal Assent by Commission Act of 1541* that required the King's permission to all legislation affecting British subjects could not be overturned by a statute enacted by a colonial assembly.

In the *Somerset* case, the King's Bench also affirmed parliamentary sovereignty over colonial legislative assemblies and slave statutes in June

1772. Moreover, the British high court also ruled "Virginia's Laws" regarding slavery were not "positive law," and Virginia's colonial slave statutes were legally lacking to allow and approve slavery within the Kingdom. This judicial ruling rendered Jefferson and Washington's putative ownership claims of Virginia-born, mixed-race Hemings and Judge based upon colonial statutes void *ab initio*... well *before* the American Revolutionary War started.

The *Definitive Treaty of Peace in 1783* was ratified on January 14, 1784, and the treaty provided that all "prisoners" of this civil war that included people like Hemings and Judge were to be "set at liberty." And without legal justification or reason... the U. S. adopted Washington's claim that black Englishmen like Hemings and Judge belonged to Americans based upon "colonial statutes." But and yet... "colonial statutes" were never legally promulgated and were rendered null and void by Parliament in 1766 and determined by the British high court not to be "allowed and approved" to authorize slavery in 1772 *before* Hemings and Judge were born. The British imperial government did not repeal the *Declaratory Act's* abolishment of colonial statutes and its hereditary slave laws. All colonial-born blacks should have been set free and, if disputed, granted a due process hearing, as required by the rule of English law. Hemings became Jefferson's child concubine, and Washington, by all accounts, took great liberties with Judge, who escaped and was fanatically pursued during his presidency.

The mixed-race Hemings and Judge were freeborn Englishmen by English law in 1773. This could not be legally disputed… as both were born the year *after* the *Somerset* ruling that slavery could only be legal in the Kingdom if there were "positive law." Only Parliament could enact a positive law during British rule, and Virginia's slave statutes had already been declared insufficient to enslave a person in the Kingdom. Moreover, Hemings and Judge's fathers were *white* Englishmen. English law of *partus sequitur patrem, jus soli,* and Virginia's colonial charter made Hemings and Judge… British subjects by birth in 1773, not slaves. These black English people were protected under the English rule of law. This was also supported by the 1656 colonial case involving a mixed-race woman named Elizabeth Key, who was granted her freedom because her father was a *white* Englishman. Yet, both Jefferson and Washington each claimed to own a legally free person *before* and *during* their terms as President of the United States of America and the constitution protected them.

Jefferson's ownership claim of Hemings and Washington's ownership claim of Judge are even more compelling indictments against these men since Jefferson authored the Declaration of Independence, which memorialized that colonial statutes were "abolished." Washington's utterance that black colonials were the property of white Americans became the dominant cultural narrative that resulted in the enslavement of 500,000 black colonials. Further, the Continental Congress adopted English law and the Declaration in July 1776... so both Jefferson and Washington were continuously bound by the *Declaratory Act of 1766* repeal of all of Virginia's slave statutes and related racialized regulations because such "proceedings" specifically challenged "the power and authority of the parliament of Great Britain, to make laws and statutes" by way of the English *Bill of Rights of 1689* and the supreme legislative power of Parliament in 1766.

Doubtlessly, the *Definitive Treaty of Peace of 1783* controlled and was dispositive of all questions regarding liberty for these black English women. They were born in Virginia, British by birth, and given the clear language in the treaty concerning releasing "prisoners," Hemings and Judge should have been freed. And if not entitled to freedom... then why not? But as John Adams had warned all of his slaveholding colleagues..." facts are stubborn" and "cannot alter the state of facts and evidence." Under English law... the *Declaratory Act of 1766* and the *Somerset* decision made colonial statutes legal nullities. The act of Parliament and the *Somerset* decision were dispositive of the legal question of Hemings and Judge's British subjecthood and entitlement to liberty upon the ratification of the *Definitive Treaty of Peace in 1783* in the year 1784. These black Englishwomen should have been "set at liberty," and if not, WHY NOT? The American Revolution did not retroactively legalize the criminal enslavement of these mixed-race women that existed due to colonial tyranny. The American Revolution did not reinstate "colonial slave statutes." It could not *ex post facto* change Hemings and Judge's legal status as British subjects by birth or alter the English rule of law.

Jefferson and Washington were engaged in criminal behavior in 1773 since colonial slave statutes were rendered "utterly null and void" by Parliament's *Declaratory Act of 1766*. The *Somerset* decision struck down Virginia's colonial statutes. Ignorance of the law is no excuse for breaking the law, and they are attributed to have known that their ownership claims of Hemings and Judge were crimes and without legal merit. Such being the case, it is understandable that the U. S. never addressed questions of legal status and conditions of black English people like Hemings and Judge or the liberty question posed by the *Definitive Treaty of Peace of 1783 before* a court of competent jurisdiction.

Jefferson, Washington, and other slaveholding Americans did not have a viable ownership claim. They denied granting freedom to black colonials like Hemings and Judge at the end of the American Revolution because 95 percent of Revolutionary War-era blacks were born in colonial America and were English citizens by birth, just like Hemings and Judge. Granting black colonials freedom would have destroyed the slave-based economy that America relied upon after the war ended. America's slaveholding citizens were enlightened and informed men of the 18th century... learned in law and politics who knew that each was exploiting uneducated and uninformed black people who were legally free and the founding generation used the artifice of a proslavery constitution to erect structural racism to further their goals.

Yet, admirers of America's founding generation are still willing to give them all free passes. They quickly point out that Washington, for his part, treated his slaves well... did not break up families, and emancipated them in his will. And

Jefferson contemplated the emancipation of his slaves as well... but sadly, Jefferson was too much in debt to do so at his death. However, the core to all free passes is the false and dehumanizing notion that the black people these men lorded over were property by law... but in reality... they were freeborn Englishmen who were criminally exploited in derogation of the rule of law during colonial times and then by the U. S. government. Thus, Jefferson and Washington are not entitled to a free pass since the behavior of an American president does matter and must continue to matter.

Hemings and Judge were English citizens by birth, and those claiming that these people were born slaves should be able to quickly point to a controlling law or an exemption of liberty rights for mixed-race females whose fathers were white Englishmen. As well, historians, legal scholars, and even school-aged children should be able to explain why colonial hereditary slavery based upon colonial statutes, laws, and racialized regulations survived *after* Parliament's *Declaratory Act of 1766* abolished such proceedings in "all cases whatsoever."

Further, hereditary slavery was an extralegal institution when colonial times ended since colonial slave statutes were never lawfully promulgated as they failed to secure the King's permission and were repugnant to England's *Magna Carta of 1215*, Parliament's 1350 statute that conferred subjecthood at birth to people born in lands controlled by the British and the English patrilineal tradition of *partus sequitur patrem*.

Sally Hemings, Oney Judge were free-born English citizens at birth since Virginia's hereditary slavery statute called *partus sequitur ventrem* was a legal nullity in 1773... as the British imperial government abolished it in 1766. Jefferson and Washington held no legal claims over Hemings or Judge *after* the Continental Congress adopted the Declaration of Independence and English law's formal adoption in July 1776. Notwithstanding, once the peace treaty was ratified... Jefferson, Washington, and many other Patriots used a pretextual claim that they legally owned black colonials and then criminally enslaved and exploited 500,000 British citizens entitled to their freedom.

In conclusion, Sally Hemings and Oney Judge were not Africans. Instead, they were free-born British citizens... born in Virginia in 1773 *after* Parliament abolished repugnant colonial slave statutes by way of the *Declaratory Act of 1766* and England's Court of the King's Bench ruled slavery was not "allowed and approved by the laws of this Kingdom" in the *Somerset* case. They were entitled to full U. S. citizenship and should not have been reduced to the status of slaves. Thomas Jefferson and George Washington's enslavement of the colonial-born Hemings and Judge *after* the American Revolution ended is an allegory for the plight of the 500,000 black colonials that America made the bedrock of their slave pool.

"Slaves cannot breathe in England; if their lungs receive our air... that moment they are free... they touch our country, and their shackles fall." William Cowper

Chapter 6
Facts are Stubborn

America has always imagined its founding fathers as exceptional, learned, and enlightened men of the 18th century. These crafted, untested accounts are myths that glorify the leadership of America's founding generation. For example... historians revere Washington for his honesty in confessing to chopping down a cherry tree and never telling lies among many claimed accolades, honors, and tributes bestowed. However, this claim that this politician named Washington never lied is contrasted... and stands refuted as it was the fifty-one-year-old Washington who first claimed in May 1783 that Revolutionary War-era blacks were owned by Americans based upon "colonial statutes." Washington's baseless claim led to the wholesale disfranchisement and enslavement of 500,000 black Englishmen and the creation of the dominant cultural narrative that black colonials were slaves under British rule. Moreover, Washington's "colonial statutes" claim is credited for the proslavery U. S. constitution, as well as the dogma of white supremacy. This was Washington's "Big Lie," which was adopted by the United States and exported worldwide.

In the book *Fallen Founder: The Life of Aaron Burr*, the author Nancy Isenberg observed that "these were our founders: imperfect men in a less than perfect nation, grasping at opportunities. That they did good for their country is understood, and worth our celebration; that they were also jealous, resentful, self-protective, and covetous politicians should be no less a part of their collective biography. What separates history from myth is that history takes in the whole picture, whereas myth averts our eyes from the truth when it turns men into heroes and gods."

The crafted mythologies of slaveholding Washington, Jefferson, and Madison have perpetuated America's dominant cultural narrative that 500,000 Revolutionary War-era blacks were owned by white Americans is responsible for structural racism and the dogma of white supremacy. But these founding fathers did not and could not own black colonials during British rule since colonial slave statutes and racialized regulations were abolished by Parliament's *Declaratory Act of 1766*. Further, black colonials who suffered as slaves to these men and other members of America's founding generation were crime victims. After the American Revolution, they were their countrymen, not their slaves.

America enslaved legally free people who were crime victims, and the revelation that America enslaved black British citizens after the Revolutionary War is a "stubborn fact." This fact destroys America's crafted historiography, and it exposes why structural racism has been resilient and the reason for the fierce opposition to teaching critical race theory in public schools. Critical race theory will reveal that most white heroes of America's Revolutionary War were ordinary, flawed, and jealous men.

Black people born in colonial America were Englishmen by English law, and America should have freed them after the *Definitive Treaty of Peace of 1783* was ratified by Congress on January 14, 1784. Moreover, this truth received powerful reaffirmation when the British imperial government sanctioned the impressment of more than 15,000 American citizens into England's Royal Navy as a run-up to the *War of 1812*. The British affirmed that being born in colonial America conferred British citizenship. The British imperial government did not recognize a right for a British citizen to relinquish his citizenship and become a citizen of another country. Thus, the imperial government considered colonial-born Americans as British citizens. Doubtlessly, and as the British General Guy Carleton told General George Washington in May 1783... the same was true for black colonials born in colonial America during British rule that did not end until the *Definitive Treaty of Peace of 1783* was ratified, which made the United States of America an independent nation.

America's cultural narrative that 500,000 Revolutionary War-era blacks were owned by white Americans based upon "colonial statutes" is ahistorical. Due to the passage of time... it has lulled most into thinking that a white country emerged in 1776 and was ably shepherded through the U. S. constitutional convention process by learned, moral men committed to the rule of law and was "a nation of laws, not men," unlike other nations. Yet, those same men ignored the ratification process under which it was established and went far beyond its mandate. Further, although charged with amending the *Articles of Confederation* to promote trade among the states, the cohort of white men instead wrote an entirely new governing constitution: a proslavery document that slavishly promoted slavery and protected slaveholding Americans in derogation of the rule of law.

Furthermore, the founding generation chose a Virginia slaver George Washington as standard-bearer and first President in 1789. Along with Thomas Jefferson, Benjamin Franklin, John Adams, James Madison, and others, Washington all are touted as enlightened men of the eighteenth century, heroes of the American Revolution. Many of the ideals that contributed to these founders' views were Enlightenment ideas but have transformed into *American Exceptionalism, Manifest Destiny,* and *Americanism* ideas.

The creation and propagating of the dominant cultural narrative that slavery in colonial America was a legal condition during British rule... and that Americans owned black colonials based upon "colonial statutes," and that black colonials had no legal rights under the English rule of law is solely responsible for the white ethnonationalism movement here in America. This white nationalist movement is no small matter. It is primarily based upon Washington's "Big Lie" regarding colonial statutes and two documents: the Declaration of Independence and the proslavery Constitution.

Massachusetts' patriot and lawyer John Adams... America's second president never owned slaves and refused to use slave labor. Before forging a relationship with slaveholding patriots, Adams had occasionally represented slaves in lawsuits for their freedom. During colonial times, Adams' wife Abigail Adams was a vocal critic of slavery. And although Adams held the practice of slavery in abhorrence... once the Continental Congress was constituted and functioning, he became a willing partner in the misanthrope practice of slavery, resolving to maintain unity at all cost, to achieve independence. Adams adopted patriot Benjamin Franklin's unity credo... *"we must all hang together, or most certainly, we shall hang separately."*

Slavery was abolished in Massachusetts about 1780... when it was forbidden by implication in the *Declaration of Rights* that Adams wrote into the Massachusetts Constitution. Yet, Adams' complicity in colonial slavery continued as he carefully withheld advancing any liberal views regarding slavery upon his slaveholding colleagues and America's founders. However, in the mid-1780s, Adams did finally share his perspective on the slavery question during the Constitutional Convention... when he stated, "[F]acts are stubborn things; and whatever may be our wishes, our inclinations, or the dictates of our passion, they cannot alter the state of facts and evidence." Adams' warning to the delegates at the constitutional convention was remarkably prescient, as these inculcating, stubborn facts have lingered, casting a shadow upon this nation's governing document: the Constitution.

The stubborn core fact is that England's Parliament abolished slavery on its soil by a general charter of emancipation in 1381, and exercising parliamentary sovereignty abolished colonial slave statutes enacted by colonial assemblies in 1766. Colonial statutes authorizing slavery violated colonial charters and English law that conferred free-born Englishmen's status unto all colonial-born people. England had by colonial charter bound colonial governments to adhere to English law and Parliament's supreme legislative power. Thus, although disembarking the Dutch privateer ship *White Lion* in chains, the "legal" status of the first kidnapped nineteen Africans brought to the colony of Virginia at Point Comfort in August 1619 were indentured servants... not slaves. After a defined period, these Africans became free British colonists. This was not serendipitous. Instead, it was because of English law and colonial lawgivers. The Africans were conferred indentured servant status even though these people arrived in chains without indenture papers.

These facts refute America's dominant cultural narrative that colonial slavery was authorized by English law. America's patriots did not and could not own black colonists based upon colonial statutes, as such statutes, laws, and related racialized regulations were lawfully abolished by Parliament's *Declaratory Act of 1766*... ten years *before* the Continental Congress adopted the Declaration of Independence. Doubtlessly, colonial statutes' inactive status and legal condition remained the same throughout the American Revolution, ending with the *Definitive Treaty of Peace of 1783* on January 14, 1784.

Virginia's House of Burgesses, Virginia's legislative assembly... first attempted to codify slavery in its laws in 1661. The colony of Virginia's legislative body was bound to England's monarch by colonial charter to a bicameral legislative system. Virginia's legislative assembly did not have the authority in 1661 to pass a slave statute that decriminalized the kidnapping of Africans, as this Act was "repugnant" to English law. Also, Virginia's legislative assembly did not secure the permission of England's King to make this 1661 colonial statute a valid law.

Nonetheless, the following year, while the Royal governor was in England, Virginia's assembly enacted a law of hereditary slavery called *partus sequitur ventrem*. Virginia's municipal law purported to make a child born to an enslaved mother... a slave at birth. This 1662 slave law required the permission of England's King, as it was "repugnant" to the patrilineal descent system of *partus sequitur patrem*. Virginia's legislative assembly did not secure the permission of England's King to make this 1662 colonial statute a valid law.

The failure of Virginia's legislative assembly to secure the King's permission was fatal to the lawful institution of slavery in Virginia. Further, Parliament's *Sedition Act of 1661* made it a treasonable offense to promulgate statutes or even suggest a "legislative power without the King" granting his permission. Yet, Virginia's practice and its legislative model became endemic within the American colonies due to British corruption.

Kidnappings and then colonial slavery were accomplished through the corrupt practice of violating the English rule of law and colonial assemblies violating the *Sedition Act of 1661* by not securing the King's permission to enact colonial statutes, laws, votes, orders, resolutions, and racialized regulations. Colonial slavery was extralegal, and reparatory justice for U. S. slave practices obligates everyone to look at the English rule of law and note that colonial slave statutes and racialized regulations were not lawfully promulgated, and colonial assemblies did not have the power to decriminalize kidnapping and slavery. Parliament abolished all repugnant colonial statutes and racialized regulations through the *Declaratory Act of 1766...* ten years before adopting the Declaration of Independence in 1776.

America's dominant cultural narrative that Revolutionary War-era blacks were owned by Americans based upon "colonial statutes" was an utter lie. This baseless claim of ownership of Revolutionary War-era blacks was first made by America's Supreme Commander General George Washington to England's General Guy Carleton in May 1783. This lie... enslaved 500,000 legally free black British colonials, many of whom fought alongside America's patriots in the Continental Army and led to the ratification of a proslavery constitution.

The colossal falsity of America's ownership claim was because colonial slave statutes were never legal and were products of a criminal conspiracy. Moreover, colonial legislative proceedings that enacted racialized statutes, laws, votes, resolutions, and regulations denied and questioned Parliament's power and authority to make laws binding the colonies. The *Declaratory Act* nullified putative colonial slave statutes and racialized regulations in 1766. Further, the grievance section attests colonial statutes were "abolished" by the British imperial government in the Declaration of Independence. And although colonial statutes were utterly null and void for "all purposes whatsoever" in 1783... this nullity was allowed to enslave black colonials when these British subjects were denied a due process hearing before losing their liberty. This false claim became America's policy. It resulted in the enslavement of 500,000 Revolutionary War-era blacks. They were entitled to due process under the law. Slave by colonial statute was America's first "Big Lie."

Stubborn facts expose the dominant cultural narrative regarding colonial statutes as being a "Big Lie." First, by way of colonial charter, as England never conferred plenary authority upon a colonial legislature to enact colonial slave statutes, in the first instance, such colonial proceedings had no force of law.

Second, Parliament recalibrated colonial legislatures by passing the *Declaratory Act of 1766*, declared parliamentary sovereignty, and legislatively abolished colonial slave statutes, laws, orders, resolutions, and related racialized proceedings in "all cases whatsoever"... ten years *before* the Declaration was adopted.

Third, the *Somerset* decision affirmed parliamentary sovereignty... then judicially struck down colonial slave statutes, laws, votes, orders, and related regulations by ruling that the practice of slavery was not "allowed and approved by the laws of this Kingdom." They can only be lawful by "positive law" in 1772.

Fourth, the historic Declaration of Independence memorialized Parliament's abolishment of colonial statutes as a grievance lodged against the British imperial government.

Fifth, the *Phillipsburg Proclamation*, an executive writ of mercy and liberty issued in June 1779, liberated and restored the subjecthood of all enslaved blacks.

Sixth, the U. S. ratified the *Definitive Treaty of Peace of 1783* on January 14, 1784... agreeing to release British prisoners. As black colonists were British citizens by law and were being held as prisoners by Americans, the government of the U. S. had no factual or legal basis for claiming differently. Enslaving 500,000 Revolutionary War-era blacks who were British citizens under the English rule of law violated America's first international treaty.

The first court-reported case of slavery in the American colonies is that of the African named John Punch, who, as punishment for a crime of escaping his indentured servant contract, was sentenced to serve as a slave for the remainder of his life. He and two white men... a Scotsman named James Gregory, and a Dutchman named Victor, stood trial in 1640 for running away. All three men were contracted to a Virginian named Hugh Gwyn, and each performed similar tasks. They felt so exploited, each risked criminal punishment in the pursuit of freedom.

Though fleeing away from their master and risking punishment as a group... the fates of the three runaways differed, as the white men's terms were only extended by four years and that the third being a Negro named John Punch, was sentenced to serve his said master or his assigns for the time of his natural life. Edgar A. Toppin, in *A Biographical History of Blacks Since 1528*, writes: "Thus, the black man, John Punch, became a slave, unlike two white indentured servants who merely had to serve a longer-term."

The *Punch* verdict in 1640 gave rise to the targeted repression of people of African ancestry within America's criminal courts. This was the first recorded judicial sanctioning of lifelong slavery within the American colonies. The *Punch* decision was not reversed, nor was it overruled by Virginia's colonial governor... as it should have been since life-long slavery was not permitted on British soil, and the sentence was arbitrary. Thus, John Punch is the "*Negro Zero*" regarding documented slavery and disparate treatment of blacks in American courts.

Slavery is based upon assaultive, criminal behavior, as the early American Supreme Court, in the case of *The Antelope*, 23 U. S. (10 Wheat) 66 (18 Mar 1825), stated, "[T]hat it [slavery] is contrary to the law of nature will scarcely be denied. That every man has a natural right to the fruits of his own labor is generally admitted: and that no other person can rightfully deprive him of those fruits, and appropriate them against his will, seems to be the necessary result of this admission... Slavery, then, has its origin in force...."

History supports those black colonials were assaulted, kidnapped, and enslaved by Americans in derogation of the truce during 1783. This was a resumption of "hostilities." A black American colonist named Boston King summarized the times this way:

America's First Big Lie

"... the horrors and devastation of war happily terminated and peace was restored between America and Great Britain, which diffused universal joy among all parties' except us, who had escaped from slavery and taken refuge in the English army; for a report prevailed at New York, that all the slaves, in number 2,000 were to be delivered up to their masters altho' some of them had been three or four years among the English. This dreadful rumour filled us all with inexpressible anguish and terror, especially when we saw our old masters coming from Virginia, North Carolina, and other parts and seizing upon their slaves in the streets of New York or even dragging them out of their beds. Many of the slaves had very cruel masters, so that the thoughts of returning home with them embittered life to us."

Reacting to these events in a May 1783 meeting... British General Guy Carleton, Clinton's successor as commander-in-chief, formally complained, labeling America's practice of mass kidnapping of black colonials as renewed "hostilities." Carleton restated the complaint directly to General George Washington and a delegation. He indicated that former slaves were free British subjects and not slaves by English law.

Washington disagreed with Carleton and responded that former slaves were owned by Americans based upon "colonial statutes." In being "property," such people were not under the protection of the peace treaty provision. Washington asked that Carleton surrender control and custody of all former slaves... but he refused, stating that he had no intention of surrendering any blacks within the realm, as all people were British subjects because of the English rule of law.

Indeed, "colonial statutes" were abolished by the Dec*laratory Act of 1766* and capturing colonial blacks during the truce, who were legally free under the English rule of law and liberated by the *Phillipsburg Proclamation* in 1779... whom which Parliament's *English Bill of Rights of 1689* made protected "subjects" of King George III before this civil war began violated the *Treaty of Paris of 1783*. Further, black colonials who suffered under colonial tyranny did not miraculously become the chattel property of the Americans upon the end of the war. Instead, as the Continental Congress adopted English law, as did each of the states in 1776, under the holding in the *Stapylton* case... putative slave-owning Americans had the legal burden of proving ownership. All 500,000 Revolutionary War-era blacks were entitled to a habeas hearing and relief. The claim that black colonials were not entitled to liberty or at least a habeas hearing under the peace treaty was not supported by the facts nor the law.

Washington's bare claim to Carleton that black colonists were chattel owned by Americans based upon "colonial statutes" was legally insufficient to alleviate the U. S. or its citizens from its legal obligation to liberate all black loyalists or substantiate their lawful exclusion from being entitled to liberty under the *Treaty of Paris* and English law.

Moreover, the U. S., in having adopted the English rule of law, was legally required to apply the same standard used by Lord Chief Justice Mansfield in the *R v. Stapylton* case, which determined that a putative slave master must prove his claim of ownership of a black person.

The 1771 case of *R. v. Stapylton* (K.B.1771) was a criminal case against a putative slave master. He proffered a chattel ownership of a human person defense to deport an African named Thomas Lewis forcibly. At the 1771 trial before Lord Chief Justice Mansfield, Stapylton's defense rested on the basis that as a slave was property... his assaultive acts against Lewis were not criminal offenses. In *Stapylton*... Mansfield allowed extensive testimony by Lewis regarding his life history as it related to Stapylton's alleged title.

During the trial, Mansfield endeavored to coax Stapylton to settle with Lewis by stating that "being black will not prove the property," and he outwardly doubted the legal sufficiency of his defense. And in the course of summing up, the Lord Chief Justice stated, "whether they (slave owners) have this kind of property or not in England has never been solemnly determined." It appears quite likely that by a "solemn determination," Mansfield had in mind taking a special verdict and hearing arguments before the Twelve Judges, a procedure which he ultimately used in the *James Somerset* case the following year to determine essential points of law. This was an *en banc* tribunal where all twelve justices of England's three high courts, King's Bench, Common Pleas, and Exchequer, presided.

History supports, no solemn determination had ever been rendered regarding chattel ownership of a human person defense in the Kingdom.

Mansfield appeared to have been willing to create a process that could lead to such determination.

Lord Mansfield tested Stapylton's title based on his view of what English law required, *sub silentio* determining the slave's status under English law. Still, in the end, Mansfield directed the jury that they should presume Lewis was a free man unless Stapylton proved otherwise. Mansfield instructed the jury that if they found that Stapylton had a property interest in Lewis, they should bring in a special verdict; if not, "you will find the Defendant Guilty."

The all-white jury convicted Stapylton. Mansfield credited most, if not all, of Lewis's testimony, not just his testimony on the "chain of ownership" issue, and very clearly communicated his belief in Lewis's credibility to the jury. And to the jury, Mansfield stated that "I think you have done very right. I should have found the same verdict... he was not the property" (of Stapylton). Mansfield's holding in Stapylton became a controlling precedent.

The *Somerset* case began on November 28, 1771, after Lord Chief Justice Mansfield denied a renewed motion for judgment by the plaintiff Lewis to have the court assess sanctions against the defendant in the *Stapylton* case. However, later that day, Mansfield issued a writ of habeas corpus to John Knowles, captain of the *Ann & Mary*, on which James Somerset, a slave, born in the colony of Virginia, was "confined in irons." Somerset had escaped... but was recaptured by the end of November and in Knowles's custody, heading for Jamaica. The putative slave master Charles Stewart directed Somerset to be sold to a sugar plantation for hard labor. Somerset's three godparents from his baptism as a Christian in England, John Marlow, Thomas Walkin, and Elizabeth Cade, made the petition on behalf of Somerset.

Captain Knowles of the slave ship produced Somerset before Lord Mansfield of the King's Bench, and the return to the writ stated the following points. There were "Negro slaves" in Africa. Slave trade with Africa was necessary to supply slaves to the colonies. By colonial law, slaves were "saleable and sold" in that trade as goods and chattels, and when purchased were "slaves" and saleable "property." The writ claimed that as Somerset, "a negro" was bought in Virginia and sold to Charles Stewart in colonial America, he was not entitled to liberty under colonial statutes.

During five days of hearing... Somerset's counsels made virtually every conceivable argument against the legality of slavery in the Kingdom. Somerset's counsels attacked the lawfulness of colonial slavery, the slave trade and proffered a range of arguments that challenged the legality of both institutions. They argued that slavery was contrary to natural law and there was no right to permanent enslavement. They argued that slavery was inconsistent with Christianity and inconsistent with inherent limits on the right to contract.

In response, counsels for Stewart argued, improvidently, that English statutes authorized slavery within the colonies and England. Alternatively, they argued, slaves who came to England should be treated as servants while their masters were temporarily in England, but their return to the colonies should nevertheless be compellable. Lastly, they argued that a decision emancipating slaves who came to England would endanger colonial slavery.

At the close of argument, Mansfield stated that if the parties chose to proceed to verdict in this case, "judgement should be given according to the strict letter of the law... without... power to attend to... compassion... or the danger of precedent... *fiat justitia ruat coelum*...." Let justice be done although the heavens fall, and Mansfield then announced that "though his brothers on the

Bench should be unanimous, [the case] required... [a] consultation... among the twelve judges..." The West Indian slaveholding interests controlled and financed the defense. They wanted a definitive legal ruling to resolve the uncertainty regarding their colonial human property interests and were not interested in settling this sole habeas case.

Lord Mansfield delivered the *Somerset* decision on June 22, 1772... which granted liberty to Somerset, holding "[T]he state of slavery is of such a nature, that it is incapable of now being introduced by Courts of Justice upon mere reasoning or inferences from any principles, natural or political; it must take its rise from positive law," acknowledging parliamentary sovereignty over colonial America.

The twelve-judge tribunal, obviously relying upon the *Declaratory Act of 1766* that abolished American colonial slave statutes and related racialized regulations, affirmed parliamentary sovereignty as colonial slave statutes "denied or questioned Parliament's power and authority to make laws binding the colonies." Further, the twelve judges declared colonial slavery could only be allowed and approved in the Kingdom if supported by a "positive law." Under parliamentary sovereignty, only the Parliament held power to enact a positive law in the Kingdom.

This unanimous determination by the twelve judges of the King's Bench in the *Somerset* case was a manifestation of British imperial power, declaring slavery could only be lawful in colonial America if the practice were allowed and approved by a positive law enacted by Parliament, but that was never the case. It confirmed that Parliament had never allowed and approved slavery within Great Britain.

The legal and binding precedent of the *Somerset* positive law holding and the fact that the founders formally adopted English law after the Declaration of Independence made "colonial statutes" irreversibly null and void, as Parliament abolished slave statutes in 1766 and colonial assemblies did not have the plenary power to repeal an act of Parliament.

Mansfield's tribunal adopted the position advocated by Somerset's counsels. It necessarily rejected the opposing position backed by Stewart's counsels that English statutes passed in support of the slave trade, or those governing slavery in the colonies, authorized slavery in the Kingdom. Also, the *Somerset* tribunal rejected Stewart counsels' argument that villeinage could provide a legal basis for English or colonial chattel slavery.

The *Somerset* decision had dispositive ramifications for colonial America. Firstly, if positive law was required to support English slavery, and none existed, colonial slavery was unlawful throughout the Kingdom, as the tribunal concluded. Thus, slavery could never be lawful in colonial America, absent an act of Parliament.

The *Somerset* decision was the final nail in the legal coffin of colonial slavery, and colonial slaveowners understood it as such, mainly accounting for the concerted and immediate attacks on the judgment after it was announced, as the positive law holding made the King's Bench's decision conclusive.

This apparent equivalence between a requirement of "positive law" to authorize slavery and a common-law prohibition on slavery were threshold arguments advocated by Somerset's counsels. Additionally, the positive law holding observed slavery in every country had always originated from positive law. The tribunal meant either statute or its equivalent, immemorial usage or custom. To this end, the holding applied to both England and its colonies, a sweeping application that was unnecessary to the *Somerset* decision if the verdict applied only to slavery in England. Lastly, Parliament had already legislatively abolished colonial slave statutes and suspended colonial legislatures through the *Declaratory Act of 1766,* transforming slavery into a criminal practice.

The *Somerset* decision in 1772 created a positive law framework for slavery while protecting the colonial status *quo,* and many scholars have concluded that the *Somerset* decision was a mixed-bag... a compromise designed to defuse the politically dangerous slavery issue. This perspective is supportable since the Court of the King's Bench could have quickly declared and resolved the case upon the basis that colonial slave statutes were rendered null and void by Parliament's *Declaratory Act of 1766*, six years earlier. And although the *Somerset* decision did not reference Parliament's *Declaratory Act* ... the decision devalued slave property and did as much damage to the legitimacy of the slaveowners' position as possible, short of an outright ruling against colonial slave statutes was abolished by Parliament in 1766. Lord Mansfield had promised "to let justice be done although the heavens fall" for one side or the other.

Doubtlessly, the twelve judges were obligated to take judicial notice of the abolishment of colonial slave statutes and knew that colonial statutes had been abolished by an act of Parliament in 1766, as Somerset's counsels challenged the legality of the institution of colonial slavery and its statutes that challenged the power and authority of Parliament were "utterly null and void to all intent and purposes whatsoever." But due to imperial political concerns... a brokered, unanimous decision was required, and in having accepted that price, none of the twelve judges were about to articulate their reasoning publicly or in any way tried to address the uncertainty on these points once controversy began. Nonetheless, the positive law holding for authorizing slavery had sweeping implications for imperial politics and colonial slave practices, which hobbled ahead.

Slavery's origins, as well as its introduction into the U. S., was inglorious and is an inconvenient truth that brings shame to the founders and America's historiography, as it enslaved British citizens upon a bare claim that such people were slaves based upon "colonial statutes," when in fact, colonial statutes were abolished by Parliament's *Declaratory Act of 1766* and was an enumerated grievance in the Declaration that colonial statutes were "abolished" by the imperial government during British rule. Further, British General Henry Clinton liberated all-black colonials suffering as a slave under the *Phillipsburg Proclamation* during colonial times.

"America is not another word for opportunity to all her sons."
W. E. B. DuBois, *The Souls of Black Folk*

Chapter 7
Constitutional Patriotism

Parliament's parliamentary sovereignty conferred plenary power and authority unto the British imperial government to abolish colonial slave statutes and racialized laws and regulations under the English rule of law during British colonial rule. The *Declaratory Act of 1766*... rendered colonial slave statutes, laws, and racialized regulations null and void in 1766. Still, slavery continued in colonial America due to the tyranny of the colonial government and the British imperial government's failure to hold its colonial citizens to account for their criminal behavior. Nonetheless, black colonials who suffered as slaves to America's founding generation were not lawfully owned and were returned to status *quo ante* in 1766.

The *Somerset* decision declared slavery was not "allowed and approved by the laws of this Kingdom" and rejected the legal sufficiency of Virginia's slave statutes and racialized laws in

America's First Big Lie

1772. This was the final straw that caused slaveholding colonists to lose confidence and faith in continuing their scheme of slavery with local British colonial government officials. Losing confidence and trust caused their profitable relationship to deteriorate, and within a decade, the same slaveholding colonists changed sides and were found spearheading civil unrest and pushing for independence. Colonial Virginians were instrumental in the creation of the Continental Congress in 1774.

This caused northern colonists with liberal views dissonance as their leaders had willingly allowed slavers into their rebellion. Without a doubt, slaveholding colonists opposed the core ideals and values of civic nationhood envisioned by northern colonists. For example, the *Boston Massacre* was marked when political tension between British soldiers and colonists became deadly in the colonies of the north, and a black colonist named Crispus Attucks was the first to fall. This was the beginning of a downward spiral in the relationship between England and the northern colonies. Attucks and the other four patriots who died that day became martyrs, framing the source of the angst.

Many northern patriots were against slavery, such as Massachusetts lawyer and political activist James Otis, who favored extending the freedoms of life, liberty, and property to black colonists. Otis' idea of racial equality also permeated his *Rights of the British Colonies* (1764)... "The colonists are by the law of nature freeborn, as indeed all men are, white or black." Otis and other abolitionists found themselves compromising their political and moral values... in favor of independence. They found the act of rebellion by throwing in with slaveholding colonials an anathema and just plain wrong.

Fatally defective colonial statutes with the assistance of corrupt colonial government officials upended the rule of law. Virginia's House of Burgesses purported to enact a slave statute in 1661 and purported to pass the hereditary statute of *partus sequitur ventrem* in 1662 that imposed lifetime bondage on colonial-born people based on the legal status of the mother. However, Virginia's legislative assembly did not have plenary power or authority to enact a slave statute or the power to change the English patrilineal descent system of *partus sequitur patrem* to matrilineal. And while Virginia's slave statute of 1661 and the 1662 hereditary statute of *partus sequitur ventrem* were treasonable offenses under the *Sedition Act of 1661* which made it a high crime to promulgate a statute or to suggest a "legislative power without the King,"... none of these men were held to criminal account.

The legislative assemblies were bicameral, and a slave statute required the King's permission to be a valid colonial statute. The King did not give his permission. As a matter of law, colonial slave statutes were "repugnant" to English law. Still, soon, this slavery scheme was emulated and respected by all 13 colonial assemblies due to racial terrorism and a British imperial policy of salutary neglect. It became endemic throughout the British colonies. However, colonial statutes were not positive laws and did not lawfully authorize the enslavement of black colonists or Africans during colonial times.

A Parliament enacted statute made blacks born in colonial America Englishmen. They were deemed **"children of the King"** protected by a 1350 **"Statute for those who are born in Parts beyond Sea."** Then in 1381, Parliament issued a general charter of emancipation, abolishing slavery on British soil. Further, Parliament's *Habeas Corpus Act of 1679* and *English Bill of Rights of 1689*, among many rights, granted due process and protection from cruel and unusual punishment... life-long slavery for African ancestry qualified.

Colonial slavery within the American colonies operated extralegally... as no Englishman could be born a slave. Yet, backed by colonial statutes and by colonial government officials... black colonials, although Englishmen by birth were enslaved in colonial America, and everyone knew it was unlawful. Further, to highlight the colonial tyranny and racial terrorism... colonial slave statutes were never approved and authorized by the laws of England, and the colonial legislators violated the *Sedition Act of 1661* by purporting to enforce slave laws enacted without the King's permission. Further, the British imperial government had legitimate reasons for not holding violators to account for their criminal behavior.

Nonetheless, Parliament's *Declaratory Act of 1766* exercised parliamentary sovereignty when it legislatively abolished colonial statutes, laws, votes, orders, resolutions, and related racialized regulations ten years *before* the Declaration of Independence. Further, it is significant... and dispositive of all legal questions surrounding the status of "colonial slave statutes" when the Declaration of Independence was adopted on July 4, 1776... that the 1772 seminal decision of the Twelve Judges of England's Court of the King's Bench in the *Somerset v. Stewart* case determined slavery was not "allowed and approved by the laws of this Kingdom" and established a Positive Law Framework for authorizing slavery within the Kingdom of Great Britain... a legislative power that vested exclusively with Parliament.

Yet in 1775... General Washington barred blacks from being in the Continental Army... and only after Virginia's Governor Lord Dunmore emancipated and recruited former slaves to fight against the Patriots in November 1775 did Congress reverse Washington's ban on black recruitment in January 1776. Black soldiers were promised freedom, and eventually, they were fighting alongside other patriots to gain independence from England. Further, in the Declaration of Independence, the 13 colonies condemned King George III and the British imperial government "For taking our Charters, abolishing our most valuable Laws and altering fundamentally the Forms of our Governments" and "He has excited domestic insurrections amongst us and has endeavoured to bring on the inhabitants of our frontiers, the merciless rule of warfare is an undistinguished destruction of all ages, sexes, and conditions."

The Declaration of Independence of July 1776 created civic nationhood... built around a vision of equal and shared citizenship within the 13 colonies. A civic nation is defined not by language or culture... but by political institutions and liberal principles, which its citizens pledge to uphold.

Immigrants to a liberal-democratic state need not assimilate into the host culture, and membership in this nationhood was open to anyone who shared those core liberal ideals and values. Civic-national ideals of natural right and those rights of man are held to be universal and valid at all times, in every place became the basis for a nation of free individuals protected equally by the law, materially influenced the development of the U. S. as becoming a representative democracy. "We hold these truths to be self-evident that all men are created equal." All signatories to the Declaration conceded their status as Englishmen. They were not globalists, and nowhere within the four corners of the Declaration are any ethnic Englishmen carved out or excluded.

During the constitutional convention of 1787, civic nationhood was transformed into constitutional patriotism due to the developing dominant cultural narrative that colonial blacks were slaves based upon colonial statutes... as the founders attempted to form a union and preserve the nascent United States. This notably led to a series of compromises, one of which was the *Three-Fifths Compromise*. This transformation was based upon the baseless claim that white patriots owned black colonists based upon "colonial statutes." Moreover, the U. S. did not make their citizens prove slave ownership claims, as required by the holding in the *Stapylton* case that "being black will not prove the property."

This threshold compromise changed civic nationhood into constitutional patriotism, an idea that people should form a political attachment to the norms and values of a pluralistic liberal democratic constitution rather than a national culture or cosmopolitan society. Americans found a source of cohesiveness and unity in their constitution, which superseded other cultural influences, forming a broader American identity with fidelity to the Constitution. However, the process of ratifying the Constitution created an irreconcilable rift in America's ideals and espoused values.

The substance of the rift involved language in the Declaration's preamble..."all men are created equal," and a mistaken assumption that "colonial statutes" made black colonists the chattel property of the Americans under English rule when it did not. Americans never owned black colonials, and colonial statutes had long been legal nullities due to the *Declaratory Act of 1766*.

The terms *The American Colonies Act 1766* (6 Geo 3 c 12) and *Declaratory Act of 1766* are not found in the Declaration of Independence. This *Declaratory Act* of the Parliament provided:

> An act for the better securing the dependency of his majesty's dominions in America upon the crown and parliament of Great Britain.
>
> Whereas several of the houses of representatives in his Majesty's colonies and plantations in America, have of late, claimed to themselves, or to the general assemblies of the same, the sole and exclusive right of imposing duties and taxes upon his majesty's subjects in the said colonies and plantations; and have in pursuance of such claim, passed certain votes, resolutions, and orders derogatory to the legislative authority of parliament, and inconsistent with the dependency Of the said colonies and plantations upon the crown of Great Britain: may it therefore please your most excellent Majesty, that it may be declared; and be it declared by the King's most excellent majesty, by and with the advice and consent of the lords spiritual and temporal, and

commons, in this present parliament assembled, and by the authority of the same, That the said colonies and plantations in America have been, are, and of right ought to be, subordinate unto, and dependent upon the imperial crown and parliament of Great Britain; and that the King's majesty, by and with the advice and consent of the lords spiritual and temporal, and commons of Great Britain, in parliament assembled, had. Bath and of right ought to have full power and authority to make laws and statutes of sufficient force and validity to bind the colonies and people of America, subjects of the crown of Great Britain, in all cases whatsoever.

II. And be it further declared and enacted by the authority aforesaid, That all resolutions, votes, orders, and proceedings, in any of the said colonies or plantations, whereby the power and authority of the parliament of Great Britain, to make laws and statutes as aforesaid, is denied, or drawn into question, arc, and are hereby declared to be, utterly null and void to all in purposes whatsoever.

In his book *The Majority of the People*, the political theorist Edwin Mims described the American reaction to the *Declaratory Act*. He stated, "[W]hen in 1766 this modernized British Parliament, committed by now to the principle of parliamentary sovereignty unlimited and unlimitable, issued a declaration that a parliamentary majority could pass any law it saw fit, it was greeted with an outcry of horror in the colonies." But this was not how the *Declaratory Act* was met in 1766. Rather, it was quite the opposite. The most reasonable explanation is the *Sedition Act of 1661* that had long criminalized the promulgation of statutes or suggestion of "a legislative power without the King."

Further, the most telling fact supporting parliamentary sovereignty is the pugnacious, independent-minded colonials' failure to protest the act... and to never call for the repeal of the *Declaratory Act of 1766*. Further, the colonials only sought reconciliation with the crown by way of an *Olive Branch Petition* to King George III in the spring of 1775. This was nearly a full ten years *after* the *Declaratory Act of 1766* and points to the fact that all belated objections to abolishing repugnant colonial statutes and racialized regulations were afterthoughts.

The *Olive Branch Petition* sought to inform the King that the American colonies were unhappy with ministerial policies, not his own. The colonials tried to arrest the deteriorating relationship with the mother country... but when the King refused to read the petition, all knew that the relationship had been irreparably breached and that his ministers, judges, and colonial governors were acting with royal approval and support. King George III was so displeased with his subjects in the American colonies, he stated to his Ministers:

> "Keep the rebel harassed, anxious and poor; until the day when, by a natural and inevitable process, discontent and disappointment were converted into penitence and remorse."

At the Fifth Virginia Convention, held May and June 1776, patriot Patrick Henry protested to those assembled that a lieutenant of the crown, Virginia's Governor Lord Dunmore was "encouraging insurrection among our slaves, many of whom are now actually armed against us" reveals the King to be a "tyrant instead of the protector of his people."

Henry's protestation was a disingenuous diatribe since slavery was prohibited on British soil by colonial charter... colonial legislatures were bicameral, and colonial legislators acted in a treasonous manner by enacting colonial slave statutes without securing the King's permission. The imperial government acted in a measured, reserved manner by legislatively nullifying colonial slave statutes in 1766. This was a calculated decision by the British imperial government. They feared a wholesale destabilization of the colonial American economy and way of life if they were more heavy-handed than they could have been. The colonial governments took advantage of the safe harbor period and were mentally prepared when the twelve judges struck down colonial slave statues in the 1772 *Somerset* decision.

The "houses of representatives in his Majesty's colonies" in America, being just one chamber of a bicameral legislative system, could not on its own promulgate a "colonial statute" to authorize the practice of slavery within their colony. The bicameral legislative structure for colonial governance vexed the colonial assemblies in all 13 colonies. This frustration was exacerbated once England's monarch signed the *English Bill of Rights of 1689*, as the monarch approved and ratified parliamentary sovereignty.

Thomas Jefferson of Virginia proclaimed that the British imperial government "by one Act they have suspended powers of American legislature and by another have declared they may legislate for us themselves in all cases whatsoever. These two acts alone form a basis broad enough whereon to erect a despotism of unlimited extent." The lamentation about the *Declaratory Act of 1766* resulted in many grievances lodged against King George III and Parliament in the Declaration of Independence. They totaled nearly half of the grievances and are powerful proof of Parliament's imperial power over colonial governmental institutions.

And because of this shared concern, the first nine of twenty-seven grievances lodged against King George III in the Declaration were:

> (1) "He [King George III] has refused his Assent to Laws, the most wholesome and necessary for the public good ..."

> (2) "He has forbidden his Governors to pass Laws of immediate and pressing importance unless suspended in their operation till his Assent should be obtained, and when so suspended, he has utterly neglected to attend to them..."

> (3) "He has refused to pass other Laws for the accommodation of large districts of people unless those people would relinquish the right of Representation in the Legislature, a right inestimable to them and formidable to tyrants only."

> (4) "He has called together legislative bodies at places unusual, uncomfortable,

and distant from the depository of their Public Records for the sole purpose of fatiguing them into compliance with his measures."

(5) "He has dissolved Representative Houses repeatedly, for opposing with many firmness his invasions on the rights of the people."

(6) "He has refused for a long time, after such dissolutions, to cause others to be elected; whereby the Legislative powers, incapable of Annihilation, have returned to the People at large for their exercise; the State remaining in the mean time exposed to all the dangers of invasion from without, and convulsions within."

(7) "He has endeavoured to prevent the populations of these States; for that purpose obstructing the Laws for Naturalization of Foreigners; refusing to pass others to encourage their migrations hither, and raising the conditions of new Appropriations of Lands."

(8) "He has obstructed the Administration of Justice by refusing his Assent to Laws for establishing Judiciary powers."

(9) "He has made Judges dependent on his Will alone, for the tenure of their offices, and the amount and payment of their salaries."

These were collateral attacks upon Parliament... but were not legitimate grievances against British governance, as it was within the prerogative of King George III to withhold or confer his permission as he saw fit. Then there are grievances thirteenth, twentieth, twenty-one, twenty-three, and twenty-eighth. These grievances were:

(13) "He has combined with others to subject us to jurisdiction foreign to our constitution and unacknowledged by our laws; giving his Assent to their Acts of pretended Legislation."

(20) "For abolishing the free System of English Laws in a neighbouring Province, establishing therein an Arbitrary government, and enlarging its Boundaries so as to render it at once an example and fit instrument for introducing the same absolute rule into these Colonies."

(21) "For taking our Charters, abolishing our most valuable Laws, and altering

fundamentally the Forms of our Governments."

(23) "For suspending our own Legislatures and declaring themselves invested with power to legislate for us in All cases whatsoever."

(28) "He has excited domestic insurrections amongst us and has endeavoured to bring on the inhabitants of our frontiers, the merciless Indian Savages, whose rule of warfare is an undistinguished destruction of all ages, sexes, and conditions."

The Patriots enumerated their grievances to prove King George III's unfitness to rule the colonies. However, from the beginning of colonial times... the colonial legislative system was bicameral with England's King, and colonial assemblies never had the legal authority to enact colonial statutes. Colonial statutes and laws enacted without the King's permission were legal nullities. Moreover, all colonial proceedings needed the King's permission to be valid. All legislators who claimed defective colonial laws were lawful within the Kingdom were criminals under the *Sedition Act of 1661*. Colonial legislative assemblies had no plenary legislative powers to enact a slave statute, and the founding generation knew it.

Bicameralism was a core constitutional safeguard in colonial governance. A bicameral legislative structure for colonial governance was memorialized in each of the 13 colonial charters and was a defined limit upon the power and authority of colonial legislative assemblies. According to English scholar Walter Bagehot, who in his book *The English Constitution* observed that "A formidable sinister interest may always obtain the complete command of a dominant assembly by some chance, and for a moment, and it is therefore of great use to have a second chamber of an opposite sort, differently composed, in which that interest in all likelihood will not rule."

Critics of bicameralism claim it makes meaningful political reform more difficult and increases the risk of gridlock since both chambers must agree upon a law. However, the enactment of colonial slave statutes, laws, and related racialized regulations during the early 1660s had nothing to do with the question of legislative gridlock. Instead, it was about furthering a criminal enterprise as the legal status of colonial-born blacks were free-born Englishmen, and the defective legislation allowed them to enslave countless English citizens. The reason by which legislators proceeded was greed and corruption of government.

Doubtlessly, colonial slave statutes, laws, and related racialized regulations were products of colonial tyranny and the imperial governmental informal policy of salutary neglect. Without England's enforcement of its law, black colonials were terrorized by their white countrymen, and the failure to protect them was institutional racism for profit. However, as colonial statutes were never lawfully promulgated, Parliament acted properly when abolishing colonial statutes and racialized regulations in 1766.

The rogue actions of colonial legislative assemblies violated colonial charters and were direct attacks upon Parliament's power and the English rule of law... a species of unconstitutional challenges to lawful governance which Bagehot spoke of, as a formidable interest of human slavers took complete command of colonial assemblies... "for a moment." But, the English rule of the law stood firm since the *Declaratory Act of 1766* abolished colonial statutes, recalibrating the ascribed role, status, and power of colonial legislative assemblies in 1766.

Commander-in-chief General Henry Clinton issued *The Phillipsburg Proclamation* on June 30, 1779... the final iteration of England's *Southern Strategy* of 1775. Exercising executive power, Clinton declared liberty and subjecthood to all blacks suffering as slaves in colonial America. England's rationale for this proclamation was to stimulate mass desertion by encouraging them to come over to the British. Clinton was optimistic that an unconditional liberation of all slaves in colonial America would turn the lagging war around. And if a large number of blacks did leave captivity, Clinton thought it would strike a devastating blow at the plantation economy and force southern slave masters to use their men to guard slaves instead of fighting them.

Unlike Lincoln's *Emancipation Proclamation* of 1863, this patent of subjecthood and liberation granted subjecthood and freedom to all five-hundred thousand black American colonists throughout the colonies/states. The proclamation applied to males and females, including their children, estimated that one-hundred thousand slaves left captivity in search of freedom.

By January 1780, and with a British victory appearing imminent, defense of each State fell upon their militia. In practice, all white men between the ages of sixteen and sixty were responsible for militia duty. But militiamen complained that this protracted civil war took them away from their fields and families, creating severe financial hardships. Still, by this time, the willingness to respond to the call to arms had waned... leaving the State itself vulnerable.

For example, many petitions charged America's colonial elite with armchair patriotism, evidenced by their noticeable absence from the battlefield. The wealthy were not bearing equal responsibility in the war effort. And Virginia's legislators were swamped with remonstrance and petitions that especially complained of the burdens the war had placed on ordinary farmers.

The United States was teetering on financial collapse. Possible anarchy loomed when it sued for peace in late 1781 and early 1782. America's treasury was empty, and France was withdrawing her army and navy. Benjamin Franklin, John Jay, John Adams, Thomas Jefferson, and Henry Laurens negotiated peace terms on behalf of the U. S.

Protecting loyalists and full citizenship for all Englishmen staying in the U. S. was a significant aspect of the negotiations. England was reticent and preliminary articles of peace were finally agreed to and signed by Franklin, Jay, Adams, and Lauren, and Richard Oswald, for England on November 30, 1782. England and the U. S. agreed to ten articles for peace.

1. Acknowledge the United States (viz. the Colonies) to be free, sovereign, and independent states, and the British Crown, along with all heirs and successors, will relinquish claims to the government, property, and territorial rights of the same, and every part thereof;

2. Establish the boundaries between the United States and British North America;

3. Grant fishing rights to United States fishermen in the Grand Banks, off the coast of Newfoundland and in the Gulf of Saint Lawrence;

4. Recognize the lawful contracted debts to be paid to creditors on either side;

5. The Congress of the Confederation will earnestly recommend state legislatures to recognize the rightful owners of all

confiscated lands "provide for the restitution of all estates, rights, and properties, which have been confiscated belonging to real British subjects [Loyalists]";

6. The United States will prevent future confiscations of the property of loyalists;

7. Prisoners of war on both sides are to be released, and all property left by the British army in the United States will remain unmolested;

8. Great Britain and the United States are each to be given perpetual access to the Mississippi River;

9. Territories captured by Americans subsequent to treaty will be returned without compensation;

10. Ratification of the treaty will occur within six months of the signing by contracted parties.

In May 1783, Carleton explained to Washington that the word "slave" had no legal meaning and that all such people were "loyalists" and legally entitled to liberty, based upon "British proclamation and promises." Washington disagreed. He claimed they were owned by Americans based upon "colonial statutes" and was property that the British could not remove from the country, and therefore, it would violate the treaty... if that occurred. Carleton and Washington could not agree upon this issue, framing the treaty dispute: were former "slaves" legally owned by Americans based upon "colonial statutes" during colonial times.

Carleton declared his intention to provide safe passage and transport for each former "slave" who desired to leave the U. S. However, to deescalate the situation, Carleton suggested that each country keep a registry of black loyalists removed from the U. S.——a *Book of Negroes*. Washington agreed. Carleton stated England would pay the U. S. their financial losses if he was proven wrong. To provide for the possibility, both he and Washington agreed to generate separate registries listing their names, ages, and occupations of each black colonist removed from America, along with the names of their former masters, so that they "might eventually be paid for slaves who were not entitled to their freedom by British Proclamation and promises."

Surreptitiously, the U. S. used a dragnet, stopping the mass exodus of black loyalists. Carleton left America with only three thousand black souls in November 1783. G. P. Browne,

Carleton, Guy, 1st Baron Dorchester in Dictionary of Canadian Biography, vol 5, University of Toronto/Universite' Laval (2003). The U. S. enslaved the remaining 500.000 black loyalists and denied them liberty and procedural due process.

The preservation of Carleton's *Book of Negroes* at the National Archives in London, England, and Washington's version at the National Archives and Records Administration in Washington, D. C. is inculpatory evidence. *The Black Loyalist Directory: African Americans in Exile After the American Revolution*, edited by Graham Russell Hodges, Susan Hawkes Cook, and Alan Edward Brown, William and Mary Quarterly, 1996, Third Series, Vol. 53, No. 4 (2011). And while some historians such as Judith L. Van Buskirk, *Generous Enemies: Patriots and Loyalists in the Revolutionary*, New York (Philadelphia University of Pennsylvania Press) (2002) have applauded Carleton's "principled defense of the black loyalists," all have overlooked the larger counter-point: what about the 500,000 black colonists who became America's slaves. Carleton's attestation of the *Treaty of Paris* violations in May of 1783 frames the reparatory justice discussion, and it is challenging to America's historiography and its proslavery constitution.

"To be Negro in this Country and to be relatively conscious is to be in a rage almost all the time." James Baldwin

Chapter 8
Intergenerational Dodge

The bedrock of America's slave pool was 500,000 Revolutionary War-era blacks. These black colonials were enslaved upon a claim they were slaves due to "colonial statutes." However, colonial slave statutes were null and void and legal nullities due to the *Declaratory Act of 1766* during colonial rule. Further, the Court of the King's Bench ruled six years later in the *Somerset v. Stewart* case struck down colonial slave statutes by declaring that slavery was not "allowed and approved by the laws of this Kingdom" and could have only been a lawful condition if authorized by "positive law" in June 1772.

Provocatively, this claim that "colonial statutes" made black colonials the slaves of Americans was first made by General George Washington to British General Guy Carleton in May 1783. Washington's "colonial statutes" claim underpins America's dominant cultural narrative and the proslavery U. S. Constitution. However,

Washington's claim was meritless as colonial statutes were never lawfully promulgated and were abolished in 1766 by the British imperial government during British rule.

This creates insurmountable and interrelated problems for America's dominant cultural narrative and the U.S. proslavery constitution. First, colonial slave statutes needed to have been lawfully promulgated during the 1660s, and, second, these colonial statutes had to sustain their lawfulness even *after* Parliament enacted the *Declaratory Act of 1766*. And while conservative critics to teaching critical race theory would like to advance the case in support of Washington's claim that slavery was a lawful condition during British rule... perhaps, the statement in the Declaration of Independence that complains King George III and the British imperial government for "abolishing our most valuable Laws" will be accepted as being dispositive, making this an unnecessary and purely academic exercise.

Further, the Court of the King's Bench's ruling in the *Somerset* case in 1772 established colonial slavery could not have lawfully existed based upon "colonial statutes." Instead, slavery in the Kingdom could only be lawfully enacted by a "positive law," and only Parliament possessed such power and authority. Thus, under the holding in the *Somerset* case, colonial slavery based on "colonial statutes" was legally insufficient to authorize slavery under English law.

Significantly, the Continental Congress adopted English law *after* declaring independence in July 1776. Thus, by law... the Americans were required to prove legal ownership of all black colonials they refused to free under the holding in *R. v. Stapylton*: "being black will not prove the property." Yet, the Americans were anti-rule of law when they enslaved black colonials, claimed them as their slaves, and did not prove legal ownership of their countrymen based on "colonial statutes" or anything.

America's detainment, enslavement, and exploitation of 500,000 presumptive British citizens *after* ratifying the *Definitive Treaty of Peace of 1783* were without factual or legal support. This was apparent since liberty was a personal right during colonial times based upon the *Charter of Emancipation of 1381*. The rule of law announced in the pre-colonial case in 1569, *Matter of Cartwright* ruling slavery was unconstitutional on British soil... "England was too pure an air for slaves to breathe in." Such was why the *legal* status of the first 19 Africans brought to the colony of Virginia in August 1619 were indentured servants... not slaves. The legal status of the Africans as indentured servants was not a matter of luck. Instead, it was that the rule of lawgivers were faithfully applying the English tradition of law. Moreover, the legal status of black colonials was the same status held by white colonials. Under English law, black colonials were returned to status *quo ante* once the British imperial government abolished colonial statutes and racialized regulations in 1766.

Doubtlessly, as colonial slave statutes questioned Parliament's power and authority to enact a law that prohibited slavery on British soil... the *General Charter of Emancipation of 1381*, Parliament's *Habeas Corpus Act of 1679,* and the *English Bill of Rights of 1689* that granted fundamental liberty rights to everyone in the Kingdom the *Declaratory Act of 1766* rendered such colonial statutes, laws, orders, resolutions, and related racialized regulations "utterly null and void to all in purposes whatsoever" before the Declaration of Independence in 1776.

Before the *Declaratory Act* was passed, the condition called "slavery" operated extralegally due to corrupt colonial government officials, graft, and colonial tyranny. The colonial government officials should have vetoed colonial statutes since colonial legislatures failed to secure the British King's permission and purported to enact a statute or law without the King's permission deemed treason by way of the *Sedition Act of 1661*. Decidedly, none of the colonial assemblies had plenary power to enact a positive law to authorize slavery. And due to the corruption of colonial government officials, graft, and racialized tyranny... the criminal scheme of slavery flourished in colonial America. The slaveholding colonists within the North American colonies were never held to account for their illegal activities targeted at black colonists, and they refused to honor the rule of law.

Parliament exercised parliamentary sovereignty, enacting the *Declaratory Act* in 1766, rendering colonial slave statutes null and void in "all cases whatsoever," and colonial statutes were void when the Declaration of Independence was adopted on July 4, 1776. Parliament's legislative authority was supreme during colonial times when the Continental Congress adopted the Declaration on July 4, 1776. The founders knew colonial statutes were null and void when they failed to "set at liberty" 500,000 Revolutionary War-era blacks after ratifying the *Definitive Treaty of Peace* ended the American Revolution on January 14, 1784.

The legal claim that "colonial statutes" were null and void during colonial times received powerful reaffirmation once the Continental Congress adopted the Declaration of Independence condemning England's King George III and the imperial government for refusing "his Assent to Laws"… "**For taking our Charters, abolishing our most valuable Laws, and altering fundamentally the Forms of our Governments.**" It is probative, if not dispositive, that these condemnations established that colonial slavery was an extralegal practice… and was lawfully abolished by the British in 1766.

Lerone Bennett, Jr. observed in his seminal book *Before the Mayflower* that the Declaration of Independence "scattered four revolutionary seeds to the four corners of the earth." He observed:

1. "That all men are created equal and are endowed by their Creator with natural and inalienable rights no man or government can bestow or take away.

2. That to secure these rights men creates civil communities and civil authorities, who derive just power from the consent of the governed.

3. That members of the community are colleagues and not subjects and that

legitimate government consists in the dominion, in short, of people over themselves and not in the dominion of communities over communities or groups over groups.

4. That when governments are destructive of these ends as evidenced by bad faith ("a long train of abuses and usurpations pursuing invariably the same object.") it is the duty of citizens to alter or abolish these governments."

These ideals, coupled with the Continental Congress's rejection of Thomas Jefferson's bill to adopt Roman and the formal adoption of English law in 1776, were dispositive legislative acts that resolved the question of the post-treaty validity of colonial statutes. The adoption of English law, followed by each of the thirteen states adopting English law in 1776… had the legal ramification of delegitimizing all trappings, relics, and claims of ownership of black people based upon colonial statutes.

Colonial statutes were legislatively rendered null and void by the imperial government in 1766. And parliamentary sovereignty allowed Parliament to exercise supreme legislative authority over the American colonies. It rendered colonial proceedings such as colonial slave statutes, laws, and racialized regulations null and void in 1766… ten years *before* the Declaration of Independence.

Parliament's legislative powers, authority, and promulgations of law pre-dates colonial times. Moreover, parliamentarians opposed the British monarchy's *Divine Right of King,* causing the *English Civil Wars* in 1642. This resulted in Parliament's *Habeas Corpus Act of 1679* and Parliament's *English Bill of Rights of 1689* and Parliament's *Declaratory Act of 1766.* The colonial government and its co-conspirators used race as its basis and are responsible for structural racism and the ideology of white supremacy. And although slavery predates written human records, slavery within America's colonies was unique since they used an artifice of law and racial division to enslave their citizens, which Adolph Hitler built upon three-century later. Further, the colonial slavery scheme was the first time a republic enslaved its own citizens in derogation of the rule of law.

The criminal practice of hereditary slavery in colonial America and institutionalized racism are binary, locked in mutual orbit with the emergence of the proslavery constitution. Hereditary slavery was a criminal scheme, and it operated counter to the *English Bill of Rights of*

1689. Colonial slave statutes that enslaved colonial-born people like Sally Hemings and Oney Judge of Virginia *pre*-Declaration of Independence specially denied and challenged "the power and authority of the parliament of Great Britain, to make laws and statutes." Further, as colonial statutes were rendered null and void by an act of Parliament in 1766... and Continental Congress adopted English law in 1776... the U. S. did not have a legal basis for refusing to free the 500,000 Revolutionary War-era blacks *per* the *Definitive Treaty of Peace of 1783*.

The history of slavery is a tale of systemic government corruption during colonial times... but a new species of tyranny and a fissure developed in the aftermath of the rulings in the *Somerset* case. The learned slaveholding colonists within the American colonies were concerned about the core ruling in the *Somerset* case. The decision placed slaveholding colonials outside the rule of English law because it made the unqualified declaration that slavery was not "allowed and approved by the laws of this Kingdom" and could only be lawful by "positive law." The American colonies were within the kingdom, and only Parliament had the power to enact a "positive law, colonial slavery became a criminal enterprise.

The British imperial government shared this perspective... and feared chaos, a breakdown in the social order, and outright rebellion if the *Somerset* decision was strongly enforced and tried to minimalize the sweeping implications of the decision. The British imperial government encouraged the British colonial government officials to downplay the *Somerset* decision. But this gave the colonies a common grievance against the British imperial government: the *Somerset* case.

Northern patriots like Samuel Adams clamored that colonial governors' vetoes of Massachusetts Assembly's legislative actions to liberate black colonists suffering as slaves based upon the *Somerset* decision evidenced England's blithe disregard for the rule of law, and it proved imperial government corruption and tyranny. And although Southern slaveholding patriots were pleased by the Massachusetts Governors' Thomas Hutchinson and Thomas Gage vetoes... they believed England's handling of the *Somerset* case when coupled with the *Declaratory Act of 1766* foretold of a nefarious plot to deprive them of their wealth... wealth created from the criminal enslavement of colonial-born British subjects, including their value as capital and the value of what they produced, even their children.

How the imperial government proceeded gave rise to ranging claims, such as the *Somerset* decision did not apply to colonial America...as the decision only applied to blacks being forcibly deported from England and attributing the decision to a rogue Lord Mansfield... who had a mixed-race niece named Belle living in his home. However, colonial slaveowners were convinced that these claims would be unsuccessful since the "800-pound gorilla in the room" was Parliament's nullification of colonial slave statutes and racialized regulations through the *Declaratory Act of 1766*. Moreover, the *Somerset* decision declared slavery could only be legal through positive law, a power that resided with the Parliament. The colonial legislative assemblies had even secured the King's permission, and now only Parliament could approve a colonial statute. Slavery was extralegal, criminal, and they knew it.

Adding to the Afro-Briton calculus was Queen Charlotte... King George III's wife, who herself was black, and their son George Augustus, the Prince of Wales and heir to the British throne. Historian Mario De Valdes y Cocom has observed that Queen Charlotte was directly descended from a black branch of the Portuguese royal family: Alfonso III, and his concubine, Ouruana, a black moor.

Queen Charlotte's bi-racial heritage troubled the slaveholding colonists, not only because she was honored by black colonials, who were convinced from her portraits and likeness on coins that she had African ancestry. Instead, England's Council of Regency had passed a law in 1765 that would make Queen Charlotte the *de facto* sovereign of the Kingdom... if her husband, King George III became unable to do his duties or function as England's monarch. King George III was not a man in good health, and Parliament enacted the *Minority of Heir to the Crown Act of 1765* in recognition that there were three minor children in line to be the ruler of England.

By law, Queen Charlotte would have all the throne's power until the child heir reached the age of majority. And only apart from some acts of Royal prerogative, such as declarations of war or the signing of peace treaties that required a majority vote of the Council of Regency, Charlotte would wield His Majesty's powers. This concerned slave masters within the American colonies, where eighty percent of the hereditary slaves lived. The *Somerset* decision had ruled colonial slavery had not been lawfully enacted by colonial assemblies.

The colonial slave masters... who profited from the exploitation of black people recognized the obvious; having a Queen with black blood undermined slavery's core rationale of racial superiority, and if Queen Charlotte became regent and head of England's church, she'd have the constitutional power to liberate black people in any colony and to jail slave masters since slavery was not lawfully promulgated. They feared the *Sedition Act of 1661* that made it a treasonous offense to promulgate a statute or law without the King's permission... a severe criminal violation of English law.

Further, colonial slave masters feared the *Declaratory Act of 1766*. The *Somerset* decision that ruled slavery was not "allowed and approved by the laws of this Kingdom" by the Twelve Judges in 1772. The colonial slave masters would have no viable legal recourse if the Queen did so because colonial slave statutes were rendered null and void through the *Declaratory Act of 1766*.

Alternatively, those profiting from slavery believed, even if Queen Charlotte displayed reluctance to forfeit the total benefit of the revenue generated from colonial America's slave-based economy, she could liberate America's native sons... men, women, and children born in colonial America and then seek to fill England's treasury by blackmailing colonial slave masters for their transgressions against Afro-Britons or taxing African slaves and their colonial exports. Everyone that owned slaves in colonial America felt that any of these scenarios were terrible and would decimate their wealth and colonial control.

America's Revolution that gave rise to this "*The Shining City on the Hill*" called the United States was more than revolutionary rhetoric... it was a movement of humankind, an eviction notice to all men of ill-intent who would pervert humanity and natural law. But after the Twelve Judges' ruling in the *Somerset* case in 1772... the slave-owning Englishmen hi-jacked America's Revolution, and though it was understood that these men were criminals under the rule of law, an aversion to Thomas Paine's penned "cause of all mankind" because they were enslaving legally free Englishmen, not Africans; yet they allowed these people to become leaders of this new nation.

In the book *Slave Nation: How Slavery United the Colonies and Sparked the American Revolutions*, the writers Alfred and Ruth Blumrosen observed that many patriots were anti-slavery and professed to hold enmity towards slavery on moral grounds but capitulated to proslavery interests for the sake of unity. However, as the rule of law officials, the Framers had a legal obligation to apply the law and could not capitulate to proslavery interests and enter a compromise to further unity and avoid disharmony. Nonetheless, for the sake of harmony, the Framers compromised.

The compromise illegally disfranchised black people who had liberty rights under the *Definitive Treaty of Peace of 1783*. The Framers assaulted the rule of law by putting black colonials *below* it and elevating slave masters *above* the rule of law. All signatories to the Declaration knew slavery was not a lawful condition, as colonial slave statutes were abolished by the Parliament and never had the King's permission. The Twelve Judges had ruled in the *Somerset* case that slavery was not "allowed and approved by the laws of this Kingdom" and could only be legal through "positive law." These conclusions mandate a recalculation of America's creed, and more importantly, its historiography.

In the late spring of 1787, the erstwhile Englishmen to the federal constitutional convention gathered for the announced purpose of reforming the *Articles of Confederation*. And in debates between May 25 and September 17, the delegates invoked Roman history, legal principles, and institutions as they debated the future constitutional order of America. Some of the founding fathers raised concern about looking to the Roman Republic because it had collapsed and became an empire. But historian Reinhold Meyer notes in *Classica Americana: The Greek and Roman Heritage in the United States* that the classics were essential to the founding generation because they were looking for "a lamp of experience in ancient history" and political thought to validate the political conclusion that they had from contemporary thought and reason. However, it was a renewed, orchestrated effort by Jefferson and others to supplant English law that criminalized colonial slavery and to protect portended rights and potential losses of status and wealth.

Jefferson, who was learned in the classics, needed to note that in Rome:

> "I am immersed in antiquities from morning to night. For me, the city of Rome is actually existing in all the splendor of its empire. I am filled with alarms for the event of the irruptions daily making on us by the Goths, the Visigoths, Ostrogoths, and Vandals, lest they should re-conquer us to our original barbarism."

He notes in this quotation that Rome fell after foreign invasions, reminding delegates that internal divisions among the Roman people significantly contributed to the fall of the Roman Republic and Empire. Jefferson was speaking to the division existing between the delegates, and the certainty of collapse, lest they pull together on the question of what to do with former black colonials and Englishmen by law.

The delegates who invoked Roman history at the federal constitutional convention supported enslaving black colonists, despite knowing of Carleton's claim of British subjecthood and the *Definitive Treaty of Peace* violations. The Continental Congress had bound the U. S. to English law and the *Declaratory Act* that legislatively abolished colonial slave statutes and English case law... that a person's birthright citizenship was immutable, perpetual, and he/she were children of the nation.

The delegates knew all Revolutionary War-era blacks in colonial America were British citizens by English law... entitled to liberty under the *Definitive Treaty of Peace of 1783*. The enslavement of the 500,000 black Englishmen would never be anything other than an extralegal institution.

Initially, the idea of an America was not about protecting personal liberty or autonomy. The essential idea, long before a modern understanding of individual liberty had developed, was about government tyranny. The need to restrain the sovereign's tremendous power has been a perennial struggle for societies as long as they have existed. There are three distinct components in a democracy. The first theme is the government's fidelity or lack thereof to promulgated laws. The second theme is the notion of formal legality. The third theme is the classic expression: "No man is above, nor below the law." And indeed, the theme that its promulgated laws limit democracy is a thread that has run for over 2,000 years, as ancient Greek and Roman civilizations' political ideas have survived through texts of history and philosophy. These texts explore ideals of democracy, republicanism, and citizenship that endured and significantly influenced the formation of the Constitution.

The effort to impose legal limits on the sovereign raises an ancient dilemma: How can the law bind the creator of law? Nonetheless, there developed two distinct strains of the notion that the sovereign and government officials must operate within a limiting framework of the law. The first strain is that officials must abide by the positive laws currently in force. The law may be changed by the authorized rule of law officials following appropriate procedures, but it must be complied with until it is changed.

The second strain is that even when government officials wish to change the law, they are not entirely free to change it in any way they desire. There are restraints on their law-making power. The fundamental import of this second strain is that the sovereign's power over enacting positive law is itself subject to higher legal restrictions. This underscores why the defeat of Jefferson's bill to supplant English law in 1776 was so significant.

The U. S. was legally constrained by English law and could not cast away protections put in place by the *Magna Carta of 1215* and Parliament's *Habeas Corpus Act of 1679*. The rule of law required U. S. lawmakers to apply the same protocol used by the colony of Virginia's rule of law officials when it dealt with the first Africans arriving on their shores in 1619. They were indentured servants... not slaves under English law. However, one hundred and fifty-six years later, in connection with enacting a new federal constitution... lawmakers did just the opposite in acceding to the demands of southern slave holding states and the citizens.

The second theme, formal legality, goes to the nature of rules... what rules are and how they operate. Friedrich A. Hayek posits in his book *The Road to Serfdom* that the rule of law makes "it possible to foresee with fair certainty how the authority will use its coercive powers in given circumstances and plan one's individual affairs based on this knowledge." This allows people to know in advance which actions will expose them to the risk of sanction by the government apparatus. A growing body of evidence indicates a positive correlation between economic development and formal legality, attributed to the enhancement of predictability, certainty, and security.

A legal system that lacks these qualities cannot constitute rules that bind officials and citizens. Formal legality provides predictability through law. And concerning this theme, the violation of the *Definitive Treaty of Peace of 1783*; Congress's failure to address General Carleton's attestation of treaty violations that implicated the liberty of 500,000 British citizens, in derogation of the rule of law, coupled with the rule of law officials unwillingness to enforce the anti-slavery provisions of the Constitution was a regime of laws with inequitable... evil intent. It was a misanthrope and consistent with authoritarian or non-democratic regimes for people of African ancestry here in the U. S. An unjust set of laws is not made just by adherence to formal requirements.

On the contrary, the U. S. enacted black codes and later Jim Crow laws. These racialized laws encouraged racial repression, systemic discrimination, and lawlessness. Their formal legality brought about a greater evil because the government anointed this practice and gave a blanket of immunity to those dedicated to carrying out these unjust laws. Vigilantism was the outgrowth of this initiative.

The rule of law can strengthen the grip of an authoritarian regime upon a group by enhancing its efficiency and providing it with the appearance of legitimacy. These arguments find support here in the U. S. when one considers the prison population, recidivism rate, and disparity in wealth based upon the people. An adequate system of the rule of law is wholly responsible.

The third theme, "no man is *above*, nor *below* the law," is core to a democracy. This commonly phrased idiom is put different ways: "the rule of law, not of man"——"a government of laws, not men"——"law is reason, man is passion" and "law is king." The inspiration underlying this ideal is that being under the rule of law is not to be subject to the unpredictable vagaries of other individuals... whether monarchs, judges, government officials, or fellow citizens. It is to be shielded from the familiar human weaknesses of bias, passion, prejudice, error, ignorance, or whim. This sense of the rule of law is grounded upon fear and distrust of others.

The inevitability of human participation in the application and interpretation of rules provides the opening for the reintroduction of the very weaknesses sought to be avoided by resorting to the law in the first place. The indeterminacy of law and language suggests that this opening can never be shuttered entirely. The standard solution to this concern is an independent judiciary that serves as a foundation for the rule of law and democracy. The rule of law means that all authority and power must come from an ultimate source of law.

Concerning this theme... "No man is above, nor below the law," an independent judiciary has been proven illusory, as it was a member of Virginia's judiciary, Virginia's Governor Berkeley, who first succumbed to graft in the 1660s and unleashed hereditary slavery within the American colonies. And although the Continental Congress adopted English law in 1776 and conferred citizenship upon all Englishmen living in colonial America... the belated Legislature could not overturn the *Declaratory Act of 1766* that abolished colonial proceedings that included colonial slave statutes by a congressional act. Nor did they try. The legacy of enslaving people protected by the *Definitive Treaty of Peace of 1783*, ratified by America's Congress on January 14, 1784, has been a blackening cloud... gathering and floating ominously in the distant future that has stained the founders as hypocrites, and the U. S., as being a maladroit nation.

America's historians have sculpted the biographies of Washington, Jefferson, and other slave-owning patriots, as being heroes of the American Revolution. But historian Andrew Burstein notes that a "biography is never an accurate record. It is a construction, a covert effort to refashion memory, to create a new tradition, or sanction yet another myth about what is past." Myths are pretty durable, and while some will claim it to be a reckless assault upon America to question our heroes' biographies, such is not the case, especially in the case of America's slave mastering heroes from the commonwealth of Virginia. They are not immunized due to the passage of time, or high office, as each man had to know slavery was a criminal scheme when the Declaration of Independence was adopted in July 1776. Lord Dunmore's proclamation of liberation in November 1775 was a clumsy, ham-handed attempt to purge England of its guilt and role as the mastermind behind this criminal scheme.

The salient facts were unaffected by England's role and motive to liberate black people during colonial rule or the slave owners' protestations... black people had legal rights and protections under English law. Black people were legally free since colonial slave statutes were null and void by Parliament's *Declaratory Act of 1766*. England's Twelve Judges declared slavery was not a legal practice in the *Somerset* case in 1772. Colonial slave statutes were legal nullities, and by the end of the war, the U. S. was legally obligated, required to "set at liberty" all black loyalists or legally justify why such people were enslaved, in derogation of the *Definitive Treaty of Peace of 1783*. The enslavement of 500,000 British citizens without conferring due process to them is America's history.

"To be Negro in this country and to be relatively conscious is to be in a rage almost all the time." James A. Baldwin

EPILOGUE

History supports, the white race was constructed in the colony of Virginia in the wake of *Bacon's Rebellion* in 1676. The white race was invented as a ruling class social control formation. Before this time, there was no use of the word "white" as a token of social status. In furtherance, Virginia's colonial assembly enacted racialized regulations that oppressed black colonials while granting privileges to white colonials. These racialized regulations placed black colonials *below* the rule of colonial law while perpetuating a race-based hierarchy that became entrenched throughout colonial America and beyond. Doubtlessly… the refutation of America's dominant cultural narrative that white colonials lawfully owned black colonials has significant and existential ramifications on U. S. constitutionalism.

The founding generation, having opposed the tyranny of England, was hypocritical and shortsighted when they placed black colonials *below* the rule of law. Founding father Alexander Hamilton expressed this concern, and Abigail Adams agreed... telling her husband John Adams of Massachusetts that "it always appeared a most iniquitous scheme to me to fight ourselves for what we are daily robbing and plundering from those who have as good a right to freedom as we have." But Benjamin Franklin of Pennsylvania had already framed their then precarious predicament by reminding them all that they "must. Indeed, all hang together, or, most assuredly, we shall all hang separately." Franklin's observation placed matters into perspective, as the rebellion had become mortally personal for all, the Declaration of Independence did not change their predicament.

The heart of the Declaration of Independence in 1776 is expressed in two ideas, government by consent and equality status. They are propositions of law and the predicate of our constitution. Core was that the English had turned their backs on their tradition, and respect for the rule of law was the principal grievance of American colonial leaders. Yet, by teaching and then accepting the conclusions of critical race theory, there will be no question that the Framers willingly compromised the Lockean ideal of human equality to establish this nation in the

1780s when it incorporated slavery-related compromises in America's federal constitution.

The opposition to teaching critical race theory, voter suppression initiatives throughout the nation, and questioning the efficacy of the *Black Lives Matter* movement by politicians must be coupled with the fact that Thomas Jefferson was alive when Harriet Tubman was born in 1826. And Lyndon B. Johnson was alive when Tubman died in 1913, and it was Johnson who, as President, signed the *Civil Rights Act* into law on July 2, 1964. This makes the case that slavery and racial repression are not so far in America's distant past.

The *Declaratory Act of 1766* is true north and singularly proves colonial statutes were legal nullities when the Continental Congress adopted the Declaration of Independence in July 1776. Moreover, the grievance section in the Declaration of Independence proves that the slaveholding colonials knew colonial slave statutes were abolished, and all are placed in a conundrum to understand how the work and compromises of the delegates in 1787... constitutionalized slavery.

Creating a proslavery Constitution in the United States was inglorious and an inconvenient truth that brings shame to the founding and

America's historiography. It used this *ex post facto* Constitution to legitimate the exploitation of black colonials who were legally free people. Doubtlessly, the coming together of the founding generation created an uneasy alliance of divergent people, and as scholar Edmund S. Morgan observed; "The men who came together to found the independent United States, dedicated to freedom and equality, either held slaves or were willing to join hands with those who did... None of them felt entirely comfortable about the fact, but neither did they feel responsible for it. Most of them had inherited both their slaves and their attachment to freedom from an earlier generation, and they knew the two were not unconnected." And in America, this meant that minorities' interests were made subservient to the system's self-interest.

Constitutionalism proclaims the desirability of the rule of law instead of rule by the arbitrary judgment or mere fiat of public officials and political organizations such as the Continental Congress. Further, Don E. Fehrenbacher, in the book *Constitutions and Constitutionalism in the Slaveholding South*, defines constitutionalism as "a compound of ideas, attitudes, and patterns of behavior elaborating the principle that the authority of government derives from and is limited by a body of fundamental law."

The shaping policies of the early republic were proslavery because the federal government institutions were controlled by southern expansionists like George Washington, Thomas Jefferson, James Madison, and John Marshall. These erstwhile Englishmen did not own black colonials during British rule as slavery was a criminal practice, and colonial slave statutes and racialized regulations were abolished by Parliament's *Declaratory Act of 1766*. Thus, it was impossible for these Englishmen to own black colonials based upon "colonial statutes" at the end of the American Revolutionary War and yet, without forcing these men to prove their ownership claims, as required by law or granting black colonials a due process hearing, the U. S. Constitution protected their putative ownership of black colonials... by increasing political representation for slave owners and slave states by way of the *Three-Fifth Compromise* in the Constitution, which stated that three-fifths of "all other persons" meant slaves would be counted for both taxation and representation. Further, the constitution limited congressional power to regulate the international slave trade, and it protected the rights of slave owners to recapture their escaped slaves. Thus, when you considered that the 500,000 black colonials were not and could not be slaves to Americans based upon "colonial statutes"... and were U. S. citizens under U. S. law, the implications upon U. S. constitutionalism are staggering.

Early colonial history supports... working together in the same fields, sharing the same huts, the same situation; one would have been struck by what can only be called equality of oppression during early colonial times. Rooted in everyday experience, there were no white colonists. There were no black colonists. These people were just colonists and racial classifications... white and black came much later. And yet, this new nation risked renewed conflict with England when the country refused to release black Englishmen.

Before 1676... white and black colonials had shared concerns about colonial life. This notion of colonials having shared concerns was proven in the spring of 1676, as all classes of colonials were galvanized in what came to be known as *Bacon's Rebellion* in the colony of Virginia. *Bacon's Rebellion* is commonly thought of as the first armed insurrection by American colonists against England and their colonial government, a hundred years before the American Revolution.

America's First Big Lie

The alliance between white, Afro-Englishmen, European indentured servants, and Africans alarmed the British and Virginia's ruling class. This caused the colonial government of Virginia to construct the "white" race as a ruling class social control formation.

The rebellion was led by Nathaniel Bacon, a recent arrival to Virginia and a member of the Governor's Council, who in March 1676... after attacking a friendly tribe of Native Americans and falsely accusing them of stealing his corn... Bacon insisted that Virginia's Governor William Berkeley finance and support a militia to attack Native American tribes on the colony's border. When Berkeley refused... Bacon was infuriated, and he began to amass a militia of his own, a mix of European indentured servants, black colonists, and Africans. The rebellion resulted in the burning of Virginia's capital Jamestown, the hanging of 23 of Bacon's followers, and Governor Berkeley being recalled by the King.

Subsequently, Virginia's House of Burgesses enacted racialized statutes, laws, votes, orders, resolutions, and regulations. The essence of this invention divested black colonists of their long-established common-law rights and transformed unalienable rights protected by English law into "white privilege."

Virginia's colonial charter forbade the enactment of colonial statutes at odds with English laws. Thereby, Virginia's colonial charter's repugnancy provision and the bicameral legislative structure of the colonial legislature prevented Virginia's House of Burgesses from enacting racialized statutes, laws, resolutions, and regulations during the late 17th century. Moreover, Virginia's House of Burgesses did not secure England's monarch's permission, which it was required to do. Thus, Virginia's racialized statutes, resolutions, and regulations that constructed the "white race" were legal nullities... as they violated the repugnancy provision and failed to secure the King's permission. Nonetheless, due to corrupt colonial government officials, Virginia's racialized regulations and colonial statutes operated extralegally in Virginia.

Furthermore, Virginia's policy of white-skinned privilege and the narrative that those unearned privileges entitled them to discriminate against all non-white people grew to influence social, political, legal, and labor systems throughout Atlantic World societies.

Slavery on British soil was outlawed pre-colonial times by Parliament's 1381 *General Charter of Emancipation,* abolishing and banning slavery. Further, colonial charters bound all subsequently created colonial governments to English law and bicameralism. However, over time, Virginia's policy of white-skinned privilege became a dominant cultural narrative in colonial America. This policy was furthered by corruption, political graft, and racialized terrorism. White colonials came to see unearned privileges as an entitlement and a license to discriminate, terrorize, and take advantage of all non-white people within the colony.

Virginia's policy of white-skinned privilege came to define and shape the social, political, legal, and labor systems of colonial America. But then, the British imperial government passed Parliament's *Declaratory Act of 1766* that rendered this white-skinned policy, hereditary slave laws, and racialized regulations "utterly null and void." This abolishment of colonial proceedings and racialized rules happened ten years *before* the Declaration of Independence on July 4, 1776.

After adopting the Declaration of Independence... the Continental Congress adopted English law in July 1776, and this legislature advanced that the only requirements for U. S. citizenship were British subjecthood and continuing to live here in America. Yet, the Framers of the federal constitution would come to claim black colonials, who were legally equal to white colonials would be counted as three-fifths of a person: the *Three-Fifths Compromise*. The Framers were duty-bound to apply the same protocol as the Virginia lawmakers used when the first chained Africans arrived on Virginia's shores in 1619; the rule of law, yet they did not, and this racist notion was embedded in America's legal systems and policies.

Furthermore, black colonials, as they were Englishmen... had a legal right to U. S. citizenship and full representation during the constitutional convention that could not be unilaterally withdrawn under the rule of law, formally adopted in 1776. U. S. citizenship and representative government were unilaterally withdrawn. Moreover, as the U. S. agreed in the treaty to free British subjects held in America, and this was memorialized in the *Definitive Treaty of Peace*... ratified by Congress in January 1784... Revolutionary War-era blacks had the legal right to due process under the law. Liberty and a due process hearing authorized by law were unilaterally denied to black colonials.

Five hundred thousand legally free black colonials... presumptive U. S. citizens with British ethnicity were enslaved, denied due process authorized by law, and then were made the bedrock of America's slavery institution. Abandonment of law evidence lawlessness proves the rule of law was abandoned as all black colonials were entitled to a due process hearing under the rule of law.

The founding generation was seasonably placed on notice that England claimed Revolutionary War-era blacks as British subjects in 1783, as General Guy Carleton placed the United States on actual notice that all black American colonists held British subjecthood. He told America's Supreme Commander, General George Washington, in the spring of 1783 that they were Englishmen, by being native sons of British America or naturalized under English law. And under the *Treaty of Paris of 1783*... they should not be harassed and must ultimately be released. Further, and in furtherance of the King's direction, he would be transporting his black countrymen out of the United States if they wanted to leave.

Despite the assurance that General Washington had given to England's General Carleton, his sovereign would seasonably address this dispute and resolve it according to the Law of Nations... unfortunately, Congress never deliberated, nor did it substantively address the question of securing the release of the detained 5000,000 black Englishmen.

Instead, the United States made five-hundred thousand black Englishmen the bedrock of its slave-based economy... in violation of international tradition. If the United States had a legal basis for making British subjects into slaves, then as a sovereign nation, it was required to substantiate their legal claims of ownership of these human beings before relegating so many people to a life of slavery. Furthermore, what militates against the notion that the United States could legally impact colonial-born blacks' British nationality was the *War of 1812*. The British imperial government impressed erstwhile Englishmen, who claimed themselves to be Americans into the Royal Navy based upon the fact that the British imperial government recognized colonial-born people as Englishmen with no right to switch national allegiance.

Each of the thirteen colonies in America was bound by colonial charter to the *English Bill of Rights of 1689* and English law. As England's highest court ruled slavery was not "allowed or approved by the laws of this Kingdom" in 1772, all putative legal claims of ownership of black people were legally expunged during colonial times by operation of law before the United States' act of absolution in July 1776. Decidedly, the fact that England's highest court ruled slavery was not allowed and approved by the laws of the Kingdom during colonial rule, all portended claims of legal ownership of black American colonists were extinguished and rendered null and void by operation of law since Congress adopted English law in 1776.

The United States adopted English law during the summer of 1776. Consequently, all five-hundred thousand black American colonists should have been released under the *Definitive Treaty of Peace of 1783*.

Under English common law and each colonial charter, everyone born in colonial America was the King's subject. Although alien residents in the colonies were not British subjects by birth, each colonial charter professed foreign residents in the colonies would eventually become "Our Loving subjects and live under Our Allegiance." And leading up to the break from England, ambiguity in the colonial charters created a debate about the extent of the authority of colonial assemblies to naturalize alien residents. As a result, every colony but New Hampshire enacted naturalization policies and laws to fulfill their growing demand for new immigrants. This went on until Parliament abolished defective colonial statutes granting naturalization through the *Declaratory Act of 1766*.

Colonial legislatures did not have the King's permission to enact a naturalization bill. Such being the case, England could legally naturalize African residents under each colonial charter. Moreover, less than five percent of black American colonists were African born when the United States declared itself independent. The balance was all native sons born in colonial America.

Perversely, Congress entertained grievances from former slave masters claiming they were financially injured by England's evacuation of three thousand black Englishmen in November 1783. Varied congressman advanced and advocated the narrative that England had illegally deprived their constituents of property in violation of the treaty and that liberty for black American colonists was a mere promise. But England's *Southern Strategy,* evidenced by General Clinton's *Phillipsburg Proclamation* during colonial times, was not a mere "promise." Instead, it was a letter of patent from the British government liberating all slaves and conferring subjecthood unto all Africans held as slaves here in America according to English law.

It was the rule of law that was controlling, as most black American colonists were Englishmen by birth under *jus soli* and the colonial charter...

no different than the white American colonists and as the *Somerset* decision in 1772 declared slavery was not "allowed" or "approved" in the Kingdom before America declared itself an independent nation, each African on British soil possessed a personal right to liberty under English law. Doubtlessly, as a matter of law, under the Law of Nations, the legal status of each black American colonist's right to British subjecthood was supportable and as binding as an article in the *Definitive Treaty of Peace of 1783* or a colonial charter.

The law schools in America do not teach students that the U. S. constitution is a proslavery document shaped by erstwhile scofflaw Englishmen who orchestrated the enslavement of black colonials in derogation of law. This approach to teaching constitutional law in America was designed by legal scholars and prominent jurists who knew that the constitution was irredeemably flawed and feared a push from the Left to have a constitutional convention that would be highly divisive in their estimation, too harmful for this country. Further, adding to their calculus is the fact that the only constitutional convention in U. S. history was in 1787, that is the subject of this renewed call for a constitutional convention, went far beyond its mandate. A present-day convention could set its own agenda, too.

The late conservative Justice Antonin Scalia of the U. S. Supreme Court stated in 2014, "I certainly would not want a constitutional convention. Whoa! Who knows what could come out of it." Similarly, former Chief Justice of the United States Warren Burger, appointed by Richard M. Nixon, wrote in 1988:

> "[T]here is no way to effectively limit or muzzle the actions of a Constitutional Convention. The Convention could make its own rules and set its own agenda. Congress might try to limit the Convention to one amendment or one issue, but there is no way to assure that the Convention will obey. After a Convention is convened, it will be too late to stop the Convention if we don't like its agenda."

Further, the Constitution provides no guidance whatsoever on the ground rules for a convention. This leaves wide open to political considerations and pressures, such fundamental questions about how the delegates each state would have and whether a supermajority vote would be required to approve amendments. To illustrate the importance of these issues, if every state had one vote in the convention and the convention could approve amendments with a simple majority vote, the 26 least populous states contain less than 18 percent of the nation's people... could approve an amendment for ratification. Or it could preemptively address the potential of ground rules for a convention being changed by making them irrevocable and could make any proposed changes of ground rules a kill switch, terminate delegate eligibility or terminate the convention. Further, there could be convention monitors appointed who approved duties would be to guaranty full compliance with ground rules, with complete immunity granted to them to protect the established ground rules and to eject disobedient convention delegates.

The delegates to the U. S. constitutional convention in 1787 were only charged with amending the *Articles of Confederation* to promote trade among the states... yet the convention wrote an entirely new governing document. And the slaveholding Virginian James Madison was a central leader that promoted supplanting the *Articles of Confederations* with a proslavery document. Madison stepped into the breach by first obliquely distancing himself from slavery by stating in *Federalist 54*... that one had to admit that slaves were, irrefutably, both people and property. Yet, the delegates knew or should have known to a legal certainty that colonial statutes were legal nullities and that all Revolutionary War-era blacks were free people. Furthermore, instead of granting black colonials a due process hearing, where slaveholding Americans would have had to prove legal ownership of black colonials... the founding generation ratified a proslavery Constitution. It made 500,000 black Englishmen the bedrock of America's slave-based economy... in violation of international tradition and law. The perspective that people born in colonial America was an Englishman by law was given powerful reaffirmation when the British imperial government began impressing erstwhile Englishmen born in colonial America, who claimed American citizenship into the Royal Navy during the early 1800s.

The historian Kenneth C. Davis stated: "Of course, in the best and worst of times, it is comfortable to think that America has held fast to the 'dream of our founders,' a dream that has inspired millions of Americans to work and sacrifice and countless millions more to come to America." Yet... while the then common American and the countless million more who came knew very little of the founding generation's actual dream, they all benefitted from their criminal scheme of exploitation, racial terrorism that their descendants and other white

America's First Big Lie

Americans inherited those ill-gotten gain guilt-free and continued those practices unrepented.

The founding generation was a cohort of learned, propertied white men who, in making the constitution proslavery, were xenophobic and committed oligarchs who were rabidly mistrustful of foreigners and wanted our president to be free of any specter of having mixed allegiance. John Jay, who was president of the First and Third U. S. Congress, wrote a letter to President George Washington stating: "Permit me to hint, whether it would be wise and seasonable to provide a strong check to the admission of Foreigners into our national Government."

The founding generation did not want foreign-born people to be President of the United States. The plain language in Article II, Section I of the Constitution reveals this to be true since they addressed a foreign-born citizen's right to hold the office of the presidency by limiting the eligibility pool of foreign-born citizens to those who were citizens of the U. S. *at the time of the adoption of the Constitution*. And while the founding generation did not define the term "natural born citizen" in the Constitution, it was unnecessary to do so since England's common law precedent defined the term to mean... "born within the dominion of the crown of England" or *jus soli*.

History supports that the 1787 convention ignored the ratification process under which it was established and created a new process, lowering the number of states needed to approve the new Constitution and removed Congress from the approval process. The states then ignored the pre-existing ratification procedures and adopted this proslavery Constitution under the new ratification procedures that the convention proposed. Given these facts, it would be unwise to assume that ratification of the convention's proposals would necessarily require the approval of 38 states, as the Constitution currently specifies. For example, a convention might remove the states from the approval process entirely and propose a national referendum. Or it could follow the example of the 1787 convention and lower the required fraction of the states needed to approve its proposals from three-quarters to two-thirds.

Grievance politics has colonial roots. Slaveholding white colonials claimed the British imperial government had robbed them of lawful property by abolishing colonial statutes in 1766 when in reality... slavery on British soil was a crime, and these people should have been fully prosecuted of the law. Due to colonial government corruption, the practice of slavery within colonial America operated extralegally in the open for a century... but when the British imperial government recalibrated colonial affairs in accord to the rule of law... the white populace complained that they were being treated as second-class British subjects while embracing unearned race-based privileges that demoted black colonists below the rule of law. Yet, Parliament's *Declaratory Act of 1766* abolished colonial statutes, laws, orders, and racialized regulations. Those ruling-class proceedings that granted white colonists unearned privileges and status were abolished by an imperial government declarant in 1766.

History supports, colonial slave statutes did not have the King's permission... and as they challenged Parliament's supreme power and authority to enact a law that prohibited slavery on British soil... colonial slavery was an extralegal practice. Moreover, colonial slave statutes denied Parliament's power and authority to prohibit slavery on British soil since the *General Charter of Emancipation of 1381* conferred British subjecthood unto colonial-born people. The *English Bill of Rights of 1689* granted fundamental liberty rights to everyone in the Kingdom.

Doubtlessly, the *Declaratory Act* rendered repugnant colonial statutes, laws, orders, resolutions, and related regulations "utterly null and void to all in purposes whatsoever" in 1766. Yet, the claim that colonial statutes made black colonials who were British citizens and legally free people the property of America's slaveholding Patriots became America's first "Big Lie."

Adolf Hitler coined the phrase "Big Lie" in his 1925 book *Mein Kampf*. Hitler described the phrase of using a lie so "colossal" that no one would believe that someone "could have the imprudence to distort the truth so infamously." History support that Hitler had great praise for America's founding generation and perhaps, it was not pure coincidence that the phrase was based upon George Washington's claim that black colonials were slaves based upon "colonial statutes." Hitler told his "Big Lie" to further his vision for Germany... and no different than the exhortation Hitler received from his sychophants Washington's cohort saddled him with the unbelievable reputation of "never telling a lie." A big lie is defined as "a gross distortion or misrepresentation of the facts, mainly when used as a propaganda device by a politician or official body. Hitler blamed Germany's loss in World War I on Jewish Germans and used this lie to turn sentiments against an international Jewry and bring about the *Holocaust*.

The German people accepted the Nazi propaganda as "truth," no different from America's white colonials and subsequent white immigrants who accepted the enslavement of black colonials and institutionalized racism after the American Revolution since they enjoyed white-skinned privileges at their countrymen's expense. The government-sponsored incentives to their targeted population caused the acceptance of these putative racialized laws to become widespread. Unlike America's Constitution, the *Nuremberg Laws of 1935* specifically took citizenship away from certain citizens and designated them as "subjects" while elevating others. They were among the first of the racist Nazi laws that culminated in the Holocaust. These laws enabled Germany to persecute a segment of its society for its religious beliefs or practices.

Similarly, the founding generation told the "Big Lie" that racism and slavery was institutionalized under British rule. This was untrue and the U. S. government ratified their constitution to protect this lie. They placed legally free black colonials below the rule of law and summarily committed them to toil as slaves. This proslavery document denied citizenship to black colonials and Native

Americans upon racial grounds and endorsed slavery by designated that "other persons" (slaves) be viewed as three-fifths of a man according to the law. But what made these race-based laws in the U. S. pernicious were the underpinnings of a proslavery Constitution and the corruption of the rule of law. Institutionalized racism in the United States has been exported globally.

Building upon this proslavery Constitution, the U. S. Supreme Court in the *Dred Scot versus Sandford* case in 1857 purported to chronicle the history of slave and "negro" law in colonial America. Yet, the Supreme Court ignored the fact that so-called slave and "negro" laws were extralegal and were all abolished by the British imperial government's *Declaratory Act of 1766* and that the Continental Congress adoption of English jurisprudence made black colonials U. S. citizens after the *Definitive Treaty of Peace of 1783*, once it was ratified on January 14, 1784. America's high court's reliance on the proslavery Constitution was misplaced, and it concluded that no person descended from an American slave had ever been a citizen of the United States, citing Article III and proclaiming they and their descendants had no remedies at law in the federal courts.

The *Dred Scott* decision, as it was later called, went on to declare that the founding generation viewed all blacks as "beings of an inferior order, and altogether unfit to associate with the white race, either in social or political relations and so far inferior that they had no rights which the white man was bound to respect." History supports, the decision was well-received by the slaveholders in the South. Still, many in the North were outraged, and the *Dred Scott* court decision greatly influenced Republicans to nominate Abraham Lincoln and his resulting election, leading to America's Civil War.

So why is it important to recognize that the British imperial government abolished colonial slave statutes and racialized regulations within colonial America through the *Declaratory Act of 1766* and that the Court of the King's Bench struck down colonial slave statutes by way of the *Somerset* decision *before* the Declaration of Independence matter today? For starters, the fact that most historians recognize U. S. slavery was predicated upon George Washington's claim that "colonial statutes" legitimated white America's enslavement of 500,000 Revolutionary War-era blacks should give us all pause. When coupled with the fact that most historians also recognize the Constitution as a proslavery document, and as Parliament abolished colonial statutes by way of the *Declaratory Act of 1766*... and the founding generation admitted this in the Declaration of Independence in July 1776... such acknowledgement should cause everyone to understand the real reason conservative politicians and white supremacists frenetically oppose critical race theory.

During the beginning of the 20th century... the United States was the global leader in codified racism... it fascinated Adolph Hitler and in no small part contributed to the Holocaust. Created in America, codified racism was abolished in the United States with the enactment of the *Civil Rights Act of 1964*. History is the study of change over time, and it covers all aspects of human society. The political, social, economic, scientific, technological, medical, cultural, intellectual, religious, and military developments are all part of history and codified racism is a part of America's DNA. There is no benign justification for enacting state and local laws that ban teaching critical race theory in public schools and to proceed differently is censorship and violates the *Civil Rights Act*.

But, suppose the reason is an ideological commitment to some noble, racially egalitarian view of the emergence of the United States in 1776. In that case, this laudable commitment was abandoned by the founding generation, as colonial slavery violated the English rule of law and the Declaration of Independence is probative of the fact that colonial slave statutes and laws had been "abolished" by the British imperial government when the unicameral Congress adopted the Declaration of Independence in July 1776. Further, although this unicameral Congress ratified the *Definitive Treaty of Peace of 1783* in January 1784, agreeing to "set at liberty" all British citizens, yet they failed to release black colonials. Moreover, the proslavery constitution was used to enslave and exploit 500,000 legally free Englishmen and their descendants.

There is compelling evidence to conclude that the original Constitution, the *Articles of Confederation*, was supplanted by people intent upon promoting an ongoing criminal enterprise, first started during colonial times. The evidence supports this conclusion as the convention process was hijacked by proslavery delegates and ground rules were changed. Further, they drafted a constitution that protected the putative slave ownership of legally free people. The U. S. Constitution was not about racial equality at all. Throughout its history, this proslavery document has done much more harm than good to the cause of racial equality. To believe otherwise leads to a significant misapprehension of our early British traditions, the legislative abolishment of colonial statutes and racialized colonial regulations through the *Declaratory Act of 1766*, and consequent distortion of what our society may stand for today.

Yet, conservative critics might belatedly come forward and admit that they are afraid of critical race theory because it can expose slavery's criminal origins, structural racism's role in protecting slave masters, and compromises the U. S. constitutionalism and CRT can destroy America's civil religion. But such concerns about implications upon U. S. constitutionalism and how it makes America look on the world stage would then be advocated by the same people who have fiercely defended the solemnity of our *Fourth of July* holiday, while opposing removing statutes of confederate soldiers who plunged this country into a bloody Civil War... while calling into question those descendants of colonial slaves who might choose to demure during the national anthem as being unpatriotic and un-American. They would be the same people who claim January 6th was not an assault on our democracy and are proactively endeavoring to stop people of color from voting and no different than the efforts to enact laws to roll back access to the vote, where there are no less than 16 state legislatures debating bills to ban anti-divisive concepts law in the classroom, with conservatives making pretextual arguments that critical race theory is too divisive and regressive... as it focuses on the darkest part of America's past and not nearly enough on the racial progress that's been made. Enough is enough.

The writer Susan Sontag wrote that "if America is the culmination of Western white civilization as everyone from the Left to the Right declares, then there must be something terribly wrong with Western white civilization. This is a painful truth, few of us want to go that far... The truth is that Mozart, Pascal, Boolean, algebra, Shakespeare, parliamentary government, baroque churches, Newton, the emancipation of women, Kant, Marx, Balanchine ballet, et al, don't redeem what this particular civilization has wrought upon the world. The white race is the cancer of human history; it is the white race and it alone... its ideologies and inventions... which eradicates autonomous civilizations wherever it spreads, which has upset the ecological balance of the planet, which now threatens the very existence of life itself."

Sontag was criticized for her position regarding American history, but not succumbing to intellectual bullying, she feigned regret stating, "it slandered cancer patients." And in response, conservative Richard Hofstadter, a revisionist historian, and public intellectual, wrote an article for the American Heritage magazine in 1970 entitled *America as a Gun Culture*. In it, he stated, "modern critic of our culture who, like Susan Sontag seems to know nothing of American history, who regard the white race as a 'cancer' and assert that the United States was "founded on a genocide' may fantasize that the Indians fought according to the rules of the Geneva Convention. But in the tragic conflict of which they were to be the chief victims, they capable of striking blows." But Hofstadter's perspective is counter-intuitive, considering Americans' penchant to tell stories to explain what they are, where they come from, and what they want to be.

It is claimed that America is the culmination of Western white civilization... the *"Shining City Upon a Hill,"* whose beacon light guides people everywhere, from the Left to the Right. Consequently, opposing views challenging America's historiography, its status and role on the world stage must be expected and constructively responded to by all, as we all know now that the version of history taught in America's schools is heavily sculpted to favor America's founding generation's heroic public *persona* while concealing flaws and human failings. And while America's dominant cultural narrative, like personal ones, are prone to sentimentality, grievance, pride, shame, embarrassment. There are countless ones... but mendacity and ignorance by omission should never make a list.

Doubtlessly, the "genie is out the bottle," and critics of critical race theory should abandon the strategy of enacting state and local laws banning teaching critical race theory. Colonial slave statutes and "all resolutions, votes, orders, and proceedings" in colonial America that denied or questioned Parliament's power and authority to make binding laws were "declared to be, utterly null and void to all in purposes whatsoever" under the *Declaratory Act of 1766* and yet the United States enslaved 500,000 black colonials and did not grant them due process, although authorized by law based upon repealed colonial slave statutes.

The British imperial government lawfully eviscerated colonial slave statutes *before* the Continental Congress adopted the Declaration of Independence in July 1776. Moreover, four years earlier, England's Court of the King's Bench declared in the *Somerset* case that slavery was not "allowed and approved by the laws of this Kingdom," striking down colonial slave statutes. America's dominant cultural narrative that white colonials owned black colonials based upon "colonial statutes" is a falsehood, and historians cannot account for how America's Revolution, considered a quarter-century of resistance, war, and state-making... both strengthened slavery and provided enough countercurrent to keep the struggle against it going.

Colonial slave statutes had no legal sufficiency during the 1780s since Parliament's *Declaratory Act of 1766* abolished colonial slave statutes before the Declaration of Independence of 1776, and the U. S. government did not and could not revive and establish legal ownership of the 500,000 black colonials detained in America. They were British citizens by U. S. law and were entitled to be "set at liberty." Inert colonial statutes could not and were not lawfully reconstituted after the *Somerset* decision ruled slavery was not "allowed and approved by the laws of this Kingdom" in 1772. Once Parliament abolished slave statutes in 1766, slavery became a crime. The constitutional convention and resulting constitution was materially compromised by its declarant that "other persons" should be counted as three-fifths of a person for representation purposes. By accepting this fact, it can help to dismantle race, racism, and racial inequity as America's proslavery Constitution was used as a weapon to abridge the liberty rights of black colonials and was operationally a proslavery document.

Larry Kenneth Alexander

Frederick Douglass

"What to the Slave Is the Fourth of July?" (1852)

Mr. President, Friends, and Fellow Citizens:
He who could address this audience without a quailing sensation, has stronger nerves than I have. I do not remember ever to have appeared as a speaker before any assembly more shrinkingly, nor with greater distrust of my ability, than I do this day. A feeling has crept over me, quite unfavorable to the exercise of my limited powers of speech. The task before me is one which requires much previous thought and study for its proper performance. I know that apologies of this sort are generally considered flat and unmeaning. I trust, however, that mine will not be so considered. Should I seem at ease, my appearance would much misrepresent me. The little experience I have had in addressing public meetings, in country schoolhouses, avails me nothing on the present occasion.

The papers and placards say, that I am to deliver a 4th [of] July oration. This certainly sounds large, and out of the common way, for it is true that I have often had the privilege to speak in this beautiful Hall, and to address many who now honor me with their presence. But neither their familiar faces, nor the perfect gage I think I have of Corinthian Hall, seems to free me from embarrassment.

The fact is, ladies and gentlemen, the distance between this platform and the slave plantation, from which I escaped, is considerable — and the difficulties to be overcome in getting from the latter to the former, are by no means slight. That I am here today is, to me, a matter of astonishment as well as of gratitude. You will not, therefore, be surprised, if in what I have to say I evince no elaborate preparation, nor grace my speech with any high sounding exordium. With little experience and with less learning, I have been able to throw my thoughts hastily and imperfectly together; and trusting to your patient and generous indulgence, I will proceed to lay them before you.

This, for the purpose of this celebration, is the 4th of July. It is the birthday of your National Independence, and of your political freedom. This, to you, is what the Passover was to the emancipated people of God. It carries your minds back to the day, and to the act of your great deliverance; and to the signs, and to the wonders, associated with that act, and that day. This celebration also marks the beginning of another year of your national life; and reminds you that the Republic of America is now 76 years old. I am glad, fellow-citizens, that your nation is so young. Seventy-six years, though a good old age for a man, is but a mere speck in the life of a nation. Three score years and ten is the allotted time for individual men; but nations number their years by thousands. According to this fact, you are, even now, only in the beginning of your national career, still lingering in the period of childhood. I repeat, I am glad this is so. There is hope in the thought, and hope is much needed, under the dark clouds which lower above the horizon. The eye of the reformer is met with angry flashes, portending disastrous times; but his heart may well beat lighter at the thought that America is young, and that she is still in the impressible stage of her existence. May he not hope that high lessons of wisdom, of justice and of truth, will yet give direction to her destiny? Were the nation older, the patriot's heart might be sadder, and the reformer's brow heavier. Its future might be shrouded in gloom, and the hope of its prophets go out in sorrow. There is consolation in the thought that America is young. Great streams are not easily turned from channels, worn deep in the course of ages. They may sometimes rise in quiet and stately majesty, and inundate the land, refreshing and fertilizing the earth with their mysterious properties. They may also rise in wrath and fury, and bear away, on their angry waves, the accumulated wealth of years of toil and hardship. They, however, gradually flow back to the same old channel, and flow on as serenely as ever. But, while the river may not be turned aside, it may dry up, and leave nothing behind but the withered branch, and the unsightly rock, to howl in the abyss-sweeping wind, the sad tale of departed glory. As with rivers so with nations.

America's First Big Lie

Fellow-citizens, I shall not presume to dwell at length on the associations that cluster about this day. The simple story of it is that, 76 years ago, the people of this country were British subjects. The style and title of your "sovereign people" (in which you now glory) was not then born. You were under the British Crown. Your fathers esteemed the English Government as the home government; and England as the fatherland. This home government, you know, although a considerable distance from your home, did, in the exercise of its parental prerogatives, impose upon its colonial children, such restraints, burdens and limitations, as, in its mature judgment, it deemed wise, right and proper.

But, your fathers, who had not adopted the fashionable idea of this day, of the infallibility of government, and the absolute character of its acts, presumed to differ from the home government in respect to the wisdom and the justice of some of those burdens and restraints. They went so far in their excitement as to pronounce the measures of government unjust, unreasonable, and oppressive, and altogether such as ought not to be quietly submitted to. I scarcely need say, fellow-citizens, that my opinion of those measures fully accords with that of your fathers. Such a declaration of agreement on my part would not be worth much to anybody. It would, certainly, prove nothing, as to what part I might have taken, had I lived during the great controversy of 1776. To say now that America was right, and England wrong, is exceedingly easy. Everybody can say it; the dastard, not less than the noble brave, can flippantly discant on the tyranny of England towards the American Colonies. It is fashionable to do so; but there was a time when to pronounce against England, and in favor of the cause of the colonies, tried men's souls. They who did so were accounted in their day, plotters of mischief, agitators and rebels, dangerous men. To side with the right, against the wrong, with the weak against the strong, and with the oppressed against the oppressor! here lies the merit, and the one which, of all others, seems unfashionable in our day. The cause of liberty may be stabbed by the men who glory in the deeds of your fathers. But, to proceed.

Feeling themselves harshly and unjustly treated by the home government, your fathers, like men of honesty, and men of spirit, earnestly sought redress. They petitioned and remonstrated; they did so in a decorous, respectful, and loyal manner. Their conduct was wholly unexceptionable. This, however, did not answer the purpose. They saw themselves treated with sovereign indifference, coldness and scorn. Yet they persevered. They were not the men to look back.

As the sheet anchor takes a firmer hold, when the ship is tossed by the storm, so did the cause of your fathers grow stronger, as it breasted the chilling blasts of kingly displeasure. The greatest and best of British statesmen admitted its justice, and the loftiest eloquence of the British Senate came to its support. But, with that blindness which seems to be the unvarying characteristic of tyrants, since Pharaoh and his hosts were drowned in the Red Sea, the British Government persisted in the exactions complained of.

The madness of this course, we believe, is admitted now, even by England; but we fear the lesson is wholly lost on our present ruler.

Oppression makes a wise man mad. Your fathers were wise men, and if they did not go mad, they became restive under this treatment. They felt themselves the victims of grievous wrongs, wholly incurable in their colonial capacity. With brave men there is always a remedy for oppression. Just here, the idea of a total separation of the colonies from the crown was born! It was a startling idea, much more so, than we, at this distance of time, regard it. The timid and the prudent (as has been intimated) of that day, were, of course, shocked and alarmed by it. Such people lived then, had lived before, and will, probably, ever have a place on this planet; and their course, in respect to any great change, (no matter how great the good to be attained, or the wrong to be redressed by it), may be calculated with as much precision as can be the course of the stars. They hate all changes, but silver, gold and copper change! Of this sort of change they are always strongly in favor.

These people were called Tories in the days of your fathers; and the appellation, probably, conveyed the same idea that is meant by a more modern, though a somewhat less euphonious term, which we often find in our papers, applied to some of our old politicians.

Their opposition to the then dangerous thought was earnest and powerful; but, amid all their terror and affrighted vociferations against it, the alarming and revolutionary idea moved on, and the country with it.

Larry Kenneth Alexander

On the 2d of July, 1776, the old Continental Congress, to the dismay of the lovers of ease, and the worshipers of property, clothed that dreadful idea with all the authority of national sanction. They did so in the form of a resolution; and as we seldom hit upon resolutions, drawn up in our day whose transparency is at all equal to this, it may refresh your minds and help my story if I read it.

"Resolved, That these united colonies are, and of right, ought to be free and Independent States; that they are absolved from all allegiance to the British Crown; and that all political connection between them and the State of Great Britain is, and ought to be, dissolved."

Citizens, your fathers made good that resolution. They succeeded; and to-day you reap the fruits of their success. The freedom gained is yours; and you, therefore, may properly celebrate this anniversary. The 4th of July is the first great fact in your nation's history — the very ring-bolt in the chain of your yet undeveloped destiny.

Pride and patriotism, not less than gratitude, prompt you to celebrate and to hold it in perpetual remembrance. I have said that the Declaration of Independence is the ring-bolt to the chain of your nation's destiny; so, indeed, I regard it. The principles contained in that instrument are saving principles. Stand by those principles, be true to them on all occasions, in all places, against all foes, and at whatever cost.

America's First Big Lie

From the round top of your ship of state, dark and threatening clouds may be seen. Heavy billows, like mountains in the distance, disclose to the leeward huge forms of flinty rocks! That bolt drawn, that chain broken, and all is lost. Cling to this day — cling to it, and to its principles, with the grasp of a storm-tossed mariner to a spar at midnight.

The coming into being of a nation, in any circumstances, is an interesting event. But, besides general considerations, there were peculiar circumstances which make the advent of this republic an event of special attractiveness.

The whole scene, as I look back to it, was simple, dignified and sublime.

The population of the country, at the time, stood at the insignificant number of three millions. The country was poor in the munitions of war. The population was weak and scattered, and the country a wilderness unsubdued. There were then no means of concert and combination, such as exist now. Neither steam nor lightning had then been reduced to order and discipline. From the Potomac to the Delaware was a journey of many days. Under these, and innumerable other disadvantages, your fathers declared for liberty and independence and triumphed.

Fellow Citizens, I am not wanting in respect for the fathers of this republic. The signers of the Declaration of Independence were brave men. They were great men too — great enough to give fame to a great age. It does not often happen to a nation to raise, at one time, such a number of truly great men. The point from which I am compelled to view them is not, certainly, the most favorable; and yet I cannot contemplate their great deeds with less than admiration. They were statesmen, patriots and heroes, and for the good they did, and the principles they contended for, I will unite with you to honor their memory.

They loved their country better than their own private interests; and, though this is not the highest form of human excellence, all will concede that it is a rare virtue, and that when it is exhibited, it ought to command respect. He who will, intelligently, lay down his life for his country, is a man whom it is not in human nature to despise. Your fathers staked their lives, their fortunes, and their sacred honor, on the cause of their country. In their admiration of liberty, they lost sight of all other interests.

They were peace men; but they preferred revolution to peaceful submission to bondage. They were quiet men; but they did not shrink from agitating against oppression. They showed forbearance; but that they knew its limits. They believed in order; but not in the order of tyranny. With them, nothing was "settled" that was not right. With them, justice, liberty and humanity were "final;" not slavery and oppression. You may well cherish the memory of such men. They were great in their day and generation. Their solid manhood stands out the more as we contrast it with these degenerate times.

How circumspect, exact and proportionate were all their movements! How unlike the politicians of an hour! Their statesmanship looked beyond the passing moment, and stretched away in strength into the distant future. They seized upon eternal principles, and set a glorious example in their defense. Mark them!

Fully appreciating the hardship to be encountered, firmly believing in the right of their cause, honorably inviting the scrutiny of an on-looking world, reverently appealing to heaven to attest their sincerity, soundly comprehending the solemn responsibility they were about to assume, wisely measuring the terrible odds against them, your fathers, the fathers of this republic, did, most deliberately, under the inspiration of a glorious patriotism, and with a sublime faith in the great principles of justice and freedom, lay deep the cornerstone of the national superstructure, which has risen and still rises in grandeur around you.

Of this fundamental work, this day is the anniversary. Our eyes are met with demonstrations of joyous enthusiasm. Banners and pennants wave exultingly on the breeze. The din of business, too, is hushed. Even Mammon seems to have quitted his grasp on this day. The ear-piercing fife and the stirring drum unite their accents with the ascending peal of a thousand church bells. Prayers are made, hymns are sung, and sermons are preached in honor of this day; while the quick martial tramp of a great and multitudinous nation, echoed back by all the hills, valleys and mountains of a vast continent, bespeak the occasion one of thrilling and universal interest — a nation's jubilee.

Friends and citizens, I need not enter further into the causes which led to this anniversary. Many of you understand them better than I do. You could instruct me in regard to them. That is a branch of knowledge in which you feel, perhaps, a much deeper interest than your speaker. The causes which led to the separation of the colonies from the British crown have never lacked for a tongue. They have all been taught in your common schools, narrated at your firesides, unfolded from your pulpits, and thundered from your legislative halls, and are as familiar to you as household words. They form the staple of your national poetry and eloquence.

I remember, also, that, as a people, Americans are remarkably familiar with all facts which make in their own favor. This is esteemed by some as a national trait — perhaps a national weakness. It is a fact, that whatever makes for the wealth or for the reputation of Americans, and can be had cheap! ... will be found by Americans. I shall not be charged with slandering Americans, if I say I think the American side of any question may be safely left in American hands.

I leave, therefore, the great deeds of your fathers to other gentlemen whose claim to have been regularly descended will be less likely to be disputed than mine!

My business, if I have any here to-day, is with the present. The accepted time with God and his cause is the ever-living now.

Trust no future, however pleasant,
Let the dead past bury its dead;

Act, act in the living present,
Heart within, and God overhead.

We have to do with the past only as we can make it useful to the present and to the future. To all inspiring motives, to noble deeds which can be gained from the past, we are welcome. But now is the time, the important time. Your fathers have lived, died, and have done their work, and have done much of it well. You live and must die, and you must do your work. You have no right to enjoy a child's share in the labor of your fathers, unless your children are to be blest by your labors. You have no right to wear out and waste the hard-earned fame of your fathers to cover your indolence. Sydney Smith tells us that men seldom eulogize the wisdom and virtues of their fathers, but to excuse some folly or wickedness of their own. This truth is not a doubtful one. There are illustrations of it near and remote, ancient and modern. It was fashionable, hundreds of years ago, for the children of Jacob to boast, we have "Abraham to our father," when they had long lost Abraham's faith and spirit. That people contented themselves under the shadow of Abraham's great name, while they repudiated the deeds which made his name great. Need I remind you that a similar thing is being done all over this country to-day? Need I tell you that the Jews are not the only people who built the tombs of the prophets, and garnished the sepulchres of the righteous? Washington could not die till he had broken the chains of his slaves. Yet his monument is built up by the price of human blood, and the traders in the bodies and souls of men shout — "We have Washington to *our father*." — Alas! that it should be so; yet so it is.

The evil that men do, lives after them, The good is oft-interred with their bones.

Fellow-citizens, pardon me, allow me to ask, why am I called upon to speak here to-day? What have I, or those I represent, to do with your national independence? Are the great principles of political freedom and of natural justice, embodied in that Declaration of Independence, extended to us? and am I, therefore, called upon to bring our humble offering to the national altar, and to confess the benefits and express devout gratitude for the blessings resulting from your independence to us?

Would to God, both for your sakes and ours, that an affirmative answer could be truthfully returned to these questions! Then would my task be light, and my burden easy and delightful. For who is there so cold, that a nation's sympathy could not warm him? Who so obdurate and dead to the claims of gratitude, that would not thankfully acknowledge such priceless benefits? Who so stolid and selfish, that would not give his voice to swell the hallelujahs of a nation's jubilee, when the chains of servitude had been torn from his limbs? I am not that man. In a case like that, the dumb might eloquently speak, and the "lame man leap as an hart."

But, such is not the state of the case. I say it with a sad sense of the disparity between us. I am not included within the pale of this glorious anniversary! Your high independence only reveals the immeasurable distance between us. The blessings in which you, this day, rejoice, are not enjoyed in common. — The rich inheritance of justice, liberty, prosperity and independence, bequeathed by your fathers, is shared by you, not by me. The sunlight that brought life and healing to you, has brought stripes and death to me. This Fourth [of] July is *yours*, not *mine*. *You* may rejoice, *I* must mourn. To drag a man in fetters into the grand illuminated temple of liberty, and call upon him to join you in joyous anthems, were inhuman mockery and sacrilegious irony. Do you mean, citizens, to mock me, by asking me to speak to-day? If so, there is a parallel to your conduct. And let me warn you that it is dangerous to copy the example of a nation whose crimes, lowering up to heaven, were thrown down by the breath of the Almighty, burying that nation in irrecoverable ruin! I can to-day take up the plaintive lament of a peeled and woe-smitten people!

> *"By the rivers of Babylon, there we sat down. Yea! we wept when we remembered Zion. We hanged our harps upon the willows in the midst thereof. For there, they that carried us away captive, required of us a song; and they who wasted us required of us mirth, saying, Sing us one of the songs of Zion. How can we sing the Lord's song in a strange land? If I forget thee, O Jerusalem, let my right*
> *hand forget her cunning. If I do not remember thee, let my tongue cleave to the roof of my mouth."*

Fellow-citizens; above your national, tumultuous joy, I hear the mournful wail of millions! Whose chains, heavy and grievous yesterday, are, to-day, rendered more intolerable by the jubilee shouts that reach them. If I do forget, if I do not faithfully remember those bleeding children of sorrow this day, "may my right hand forget her cunning, and may my tongue cleave to the roof of my mouth!" To forget them, to pass lightly over their wrongs, and to chime in with the popular theme, would be treason most scandalous and shocking, and would make me a reproach before God and the world. My subject, then fellow-citizens, is AMERICAN SLAVERY. I shall see, this day, and its popular characteristics, from the slave's point of view. Standing, there, identified with the American bondman, making his wrongs mine, I do not hesitate to declare, with all my soul, that the character and conduct of this nation never looked blacker to me than on this 4th of July! Whether we turn to the declarations of the past, or to the professions of the present, the conduct of the nation seems equally hideous and revolting. America is false to the past, false to the present, and solemnly binds herself to be false to the future. Standing with God and the crushed and bleeding slave on this occasion, I will, in the name of humanity which is outraged, in the name of liberty which is fettered, in the name of the constitution and the Bible, which are disregarded and trampled upon, dare to call in question and to denounce, with all the emphasis I can command, everything that serves to perpetuate slavery — the great sin and shame of America! "I will not equivocate; I will not excuse;" I will use the severest language I can command; and yet not one word shall escape me that any man, whose judgment is not blinded by prejudice, or who is not at heart a slaveholder, shall not confess to be right and just.

But I fancy I hear some one of my audience say, it is just in this circumstance that you and your brother abolitionists fail to make a favorable impression on the public mind. Would you argue more, and denounce less, would you persuade more, and rebuke less, your cause would be much more likely to succeed. But, I submit, where all is plain there is nothing to be argued. What point in the anti-slavery creed would you have me argue? On what branch of the subject do the people of this country need light? Must I undertake to prove that the slave is a man? That point is conceded already. Nobody doubts it. The slaveholders themselves acknowledge it in the enactment of laws for their government. They acknowledge it when they punish disobedience on the part of the slave. There are seventy-two crimes in the State of Virginia, which, if committed by a black man, (no matter how ignorant he be), subject him to the punishment of death; while only two of the same crimes will subject a white man to the like punishment. What is this but the acknowledgement that the slave is a moral, intellectual and responsible being? The manhood of the slave is conceded. It is admitted in the fact that Southern statute books are covered with enactments forbidding, under severe fines and penalties, the teaching of the slave to read or to write. When you can point to any such laws, in reference to the beasts of the field, then I may consent to argue the manhood of the slave. When the dogs in your streets, when the fowls of the air, when the cattle on your hills, when the fish of the sea, and the reptiles that crawl, shall be unable to distinguish the slave from a brute, *then* will I argue with you that the slave is a man!

For the present, it is enough to affirm the equal manhood of the Negro race. Is it not astonishing

that, while we are ploughing, planting and reaping, using all kinds of mechanical tools, erecting houses, constructing bridges, building ships, working in metals of brass, iron, copper, silver and gold; that, while we are reading, writing and cyphering, acting as clerks, merchants and secretaries, having among us lawyers, doctors, ministers, poets, authors, editors, orators and teachers; that, while we are engaged in all manner of enterprises common to other men, digging gold in California, capturing the whale in the Pacific, feeding sheep and cattle on the hill-side, living, moving, acting, thinking, planning, living in families as husbands, wives and children, and, above all, confessing and worshipping the Christian's God, and looking hopefully for life and immortality beyond the grave,
we are called upon to prove that we are men!

Would you have me argue that man is entitled to liberty? that he is the rightful owner of his own body? You have already declared it. Must I argue the wrongfulness of slavery? Is that a question for Republicans? Is it to be settled by the rules of logic and argumentation, as a matter beset with great difficulty, involving a doubtful application of the principle of justice, hard to be understood? How should I look to-day, in the presence of Americans, dividing, and subdividing a discourse, to show that men have a natural right to freedom? speaking of it relatively, and positively, negatively, and affirmatively. To do so, would be to make myself ridiculous, and to offer an insult to your understanding. — There is not a man beneath the canopy of heaven, that does not know that slavery is wrong *for him*.

What, am I to argue that it is wrong to make men brutes, to rob them of their liberty, to work them without wages, to keep them ignorant of their relations to their fellow men, to beat them with sticks, to flay their flesh with the lash, to load their limbs with irons, to hunt them with dogs, to sell them at auction, to sunder their families, to knock out their teeth, to bum their flesh, to starve them into obedience and submission to their masters? Must I argue that a system thus marked with blood, and stained with pollution, is *wrong*? No! I will not. I have better employments for my time and strength than such arguments would imply.

What, then, remains to be argued? Is it that slavery is not divine; that God did not establish it; that our doctors of divinity are mistaken? There is blasphemy in the thought. That which is inhuman, cannot be divine! Who can reason on such a proposition? They that can, may; I cannot. The time for such argument is passed.
At a time like this, scorching irony, not convincing argument, is needed. O! had I the ability, and could I reach the nation's ear, I would, to-day, pour out a fiery stream of biting ridicule, blasting reproach, withering sarcasm, and stern rebuke. For it is not light that is needed, but fire; it is not the gentle shower, but thunder. We need the storm, the whirlwind, and the earthquake. The feeling of the nation must be quickened; the conscience of the nation must be roused; the propriety of the nation must be startled; the hypocrisy of the nation must be exposed; and its crimes against God and man must be proclaimed and denounced.

Larry Kenneth Alexander

What, to the American slave, is your 4th of July? I answer: a day that reveals to him, more than all other days in the year, the gross injustice and cruelty to which he is the constant victim. To him, your celebration is a sham; your boasted liberty, an unholy license; your national greatness, swelling vanity; your sounds of rejoicing are empty and heartless; your denunciations of tyrants, brass fronted impudence; your shouts of liberty and equality, hollow mockery; your prayers and hymns, your sermons and thanksgivings, with all your religious parade, and solemnity, are, to him, mere bombast, fraud, deception, impiety, and hypocrisy — a thin veil to cover up crimes which would disgrace a nation of savages. There is not a nation on the earth guilty of practices, more shocking and bloody, than are the people of these United States, at this very hour. Go where you may, search where you will, roam through all the monarchies and despotisms of the old world, travel through South America, search out every abuse, and when you have found the last, lay your facts by the side of the everyday practices of this nation, and you will say with me, that, for revolting barbarity and shameless hypocrisy, America reigns without a rival.

Take the American slave-trade, which, we are told by the papers, is especially prosperous just now. Ex-Senator Benton tells us that the price of men was never higher than now. He mentions the fact to show that slavery is in no danger. This trade is one of the peculiarities of American institutions. It is carried on in all the large towns and cities in one-half of this confederacy; and millions are pocketed every year, by dealers in this horrid traffic. In several states, this trade is a chief source of wealth. It is called (in contradistinction to the foreign slave-trade) "*the internal slave trade.*" It is, probably, called so, too, in order to divert from it the horror with which the foreign slave-trade is contemplated. That trade has long since been denounced by this government, as piracy. It has been denounced with burning words, from the high places of the nation, as an execrable traffic. To arrest it, to put an end to it, this nation keeps a squadron, at immense cost, on the coast of Africa. Everywhere, in this country, it is safe to speak of this foreign slave-trade, as a most inhuman traffic, opposed alike to the laws of God and of man. The duty to extirpate and destroy it, is admitted even by our DOCTORS OF DIVINITY. In order to put an end to it, some of these last have consented that their colored brethren (nominally free) should leave this country, and establish themselves on the western coast of Africa! It is, however, a notable fact that, while so much execration is poured out by Americans upon those engaged in the foreign slave-trade, the men engaged in the slave-trade between the states pass without condemnation, and their business is deemed honorable.

Behold the practical operation of this internal slave-trade, the American slave-trade, sustained by American politics and America religion. Here you will see men and women reared like swine for the market. You know what is a swine-drover? I will show you a man-drover. They inhabit all our Southern States. They perambulate the country, and crowd the highways of the nation, with droves of human stock. You will see one of these human flesh-jobbers, armed with pistol, whip and bowie knife, driving a company of a hundred men, women, and children, from the Potomac to the slave market at New Orleans. These wretched people are to be sold singly, or in lots, to suit purchasers. They are food for the cotton-field, and the deadly sugar-mill. Mark the sad procession, as it moves wearily along, and the inhuman wretch who drives them. Hear his savage yells and his blood-chilling oaths, as he hurries on his affrighted captives! There, see the old man, with locks thinned and gray. Cast one glance, if you please, upon that young mother, whose shoulders are bare to the scorching sun, her briny tears falling on the brow of the babe in her arms. See, too, that girl of thirteen, weeping, *yes*! weeping, as she thinks of the mother from whom she has been torn! The drove moves tardily. Heat and sorrow have nearly consumed their strength; suddenly you hear a quick snap, like the discharge of a rifle; the fetters clank, and the chain rattles simultaneously; your ears are saluted with a scream, that seems to have torn its way to the center of your soul! The crack you heard, was the sound of the slave-whip; the scream you heard, was from the woman you saw with the babe. Her speed had faltered under the weight of her child and her chains! that gash on her shoulder tells her to move on. Follow the drove to New Orleans. Attend the auction; see men examined like horses; see the forms of women rudely and brutally exposed to the shocking gaze of American slave-buyers. See this drove sold and separated forever; and never forget the deep, sad sobs that arose from that scattered multitude. Tell me citizens, WHERE, under the sun, you can witness a spectacle more fiendish and shocking. Yet this is but a glance at the American slave-trade, as it exists, at this moment, in the ruling part of the United States.

I was born amid such sights and scenes. To me the American slave-trade is a terrible reality. When a child, my soul was often pierced with a sense of its horrors. I lived on Philpot Street, Fell's Point, Baltimore, and have watched from the wharves, the slave ships in the Basin, anchored from the shore, with their cargoes of human flesh, waiting for favorable winds to waft them down the Chesapeake. There was, at that time, a grand slave mart kept at the head of Pratt Street, by Austin Woldfolk. His agents were sent into every town and county in Maryland, announcing their arrival, through the papers, and on flaming "*hand-bills*," headed CASH FOR NEGROES. These men were generally well-dressed men, and very captivating in their manners. Ever ready to drink, to treat, and to gamble. The fate of many a slave has depended upon the turn of a single card; and many a child has been snatched from the arms of its mother by bargains arranged in a state of brutal drunkenness.

The flesh-mongers gather up their victims by dozens, and drive them, chained, to the general depot at Baltimore. When a sufficient number have been collected here, a ship is chartered, for the purpose of conveying the forlorn crew to Mobile, or to New Orleans. From the slave prison to the ship, they are usually driven in the darkness of night; for since the antislavery agitation, a certain caution is observed.

In the deep still darkness of midnight, I have been often aroused by the dead heavy footsteps, and the piteous cries of the chained gangs that passed our door. The anguish of my boyish heart was intense; and I was often consoled, when speaking to my mistress in the morning, to hear her say that the custom was very wicked; that she hated to hear the rattle of the chains, and the heartrending cries. I was glad to find one who sympathized with me in my horror.

Fellow-citizens, this murderous traffic is, to-day, in active operation in this boasted republic. In the solitude of my spirit, I see clouds of dust raised on the highways of the South; I see the bleeding footsteps; I hear the doleful wail of fettered humanity, on the way to the slave-markets, where the victims are to be sold like *horses*, *sheep*, and *swine*, knocked off to the highest bidder. There I see the tenderest ties ruthlessly broken, to gratify the lust, caprice and rapacity of the buyers and sellers of men. My soul sickens at the sight.

> *Is this the land your Fathers loved,*
> *The freedom which they toiled to win?*
> *Is this the earth whereon they moved?*
> *Are these the graves they slumber in?*

But a still more inhuman, disgraceful, and scandalous state of things remains to be presented. By an act of the American Congress, not yet two years old, slavery has been nationalized in its most horrible and revolting form. By that act, Mason and Dixon's line has been obliterated; New York has become as Virginia; and the power to hold, hunt, and sell men, women, and children as slaves remains no longer a mere state institution, but is now an institution of the whole United States. The power is co-extensive with the Star-

Spangled Banner and American Christianity. Where these go, may also go the merciless slave-hunter. Where these are, man is not sacred. He is a bird for the sportsman's gun. By that most foul and fiendish of all human decrees, the liberty and person of every man are put in peril. Your broad republican domain is hunting ground for *men*. Not for thieves and robbers, enemies of society, merely, but for men guilty of no crime. Your lawmakers have commanded all good citizens to engage in this hellish sport. Your President, your Secretary of State, our *lords*, *nobles*, and ecclesiastics, enforce, as a duty you owe to your free and glorious country, and to your God, that you do this accursed thing. Not fewer than forty Americans have, within the past two years, been hunted down and, without a moment's warning, hurried away in chains, and consigned to slavery and excruciating torture. Some of these have had wives and children, dependent on them for bread; but of this, no account was made. The right of the hunter to his prey stands superior to the right of marriage, and to *all* rights in this republic, the rights of God included! For black men there are neither law, justice, humanity, not religion. The Fugitive Slave *Law* makes mercy to them a crime; and bribes the judge who tries them. An American judge gets ten-dollars for every victim he consigns to slavery, and five, when he fails to do so. The oath of any two villains is sufficient, under this hell-black enactment, to send the most pious and exemplary black man into the remorseless jaws of slavery! His own testimony is nothing. He can bring no witnesses for himself. The minister of American justice is bound by the law to hear but *one* side; and *that* side, is the side of the oppressor. Let this damning fact be perpetually told. Let it be thundered around the world, that, in tyrant-killing, king-hating, people-loving, democratic, Christian America, the seats of justice are filled with judges, who hold their offices under an open and palpable *bribe*, and are bound, in deciding in the case of a man's liberty, *hear only his accusers*!

In glaring violation of justice, in shameless disregard of the forms of administering law, in cunning arrangement to entrap the defenseless, and in diabolical intent, this *Fugitive Slave Law* stands alone in the annals of tyrannical legislation. I doubt if there be another nation on the globe, having the brass and the baseness to put such a law on the statute-book. If any man in this assembly thinks differently from me in this matter, and feels able to disprove my statements, I will gladly confront him at any suitable time and place he may select.

I take this law to be one of the grossest infringements of Christian Liberty, and, if the churches and ministers of our country were not stupidly blind, or most wickedly indifferent, they, too, would so regard it.

At the very moment that they are thanking God for the enjoyment of civil and religious liberty, and for the right to worship God according to the dictates of their own consciences, they are utterly silent in respect to a law which robs religion of its chief significance, and makes it utterly worthless to a world lying in wickedness. Did this law concern the "*mint, anise, and cumin*" — abridge the right to sing psalms, to partake of the sacrament, or to engage in any of the ceremonies of religion, it would be smitten by the thunder of a thousand pulpits. A general shout would go up from the church, demanding *repeal, repeal, instant repeal!* — And it would go hard with that politician who presumed to solicit the votes of the people without inscribing this motto on his banner. Further, if this demand were not complied with, another Scotland would be added to the history of religious liberty, and the stern old Covenanters would be thrown into the shade. A John Knox would be seen at every church door, and heard from every pulpit, and Fillmore would have no more quarter than was shown by Knox, to the beautiful, but treacherous queen Mary of Scotland. The fact that the church of our country, (with fractional exceptions), does not esteem "the Fugitive Slave Law" as a declaration of war against religious liberty, implies that that church regards religion simply as a form of worship, an empty ceremony, and *not* a vital principle, requiring active benevolence, justice, love and good will towards man. It esteems sacrifice above mercy; psalm-singing above right doing; solemn meetings above practical righteousness. A worship that can be conducted by persons who refuse to give shelter to the houseless, to give bread to the hungry, clothing to the naked, and who enjoin obedience to a law forbidding these acts of mercy, is a curse, not a blessing to mankind. The Bible addresses all such persons as "scribes, Pharisees, hypocrites, who pay tithe of *mint, anise,* and *cumin,* and have omitted the weightier matters of the law, judgment, mercy and faith."

But the church of this country is not only indifferent to the wrongs of the slave, it actually takes sides with the oppressors. It has made itself the bulwark of American slavery, and the shield of American slave-hunters. Many of its most eloquent Divines. who stand as the very lights of the church, have shamelessly given the sanction of religion and the Bible to the whole slave system. They have taught that man may, properly, be a slave; that the relation of master and slave is ordained of God; that to send back an escaped bondman to his master is clearly the duty of all the followers of the Lord Jesus Christ; and this horrible blasphemy is palmed off upon the world for Christianity.

For my part, I would say, welcome infidelity! welcome atheism! welcome anything! in preference to the gospel, *as preached by those Divines*! They convert the very name of religion into an engine of tyranny, and barbarous cruelty, and serve to confirm more infidels, in this age, than all the infidel writings of Thomas Paine, Voltaire, and Bolingbroke, put together, have done! These ministers make religion a cold and flinty-hearted thing, having neither principles of right action, nor bowels of compassion. They strip the love of God of its beauty, and leave the throng of religion a huge, horrible, repulsive form. It is a religion for oppressors, tyrants, man-stealers, and *thugs*. It is not that "*pure and undefiled religion*" which is from above, and which is "*first pure, then peaceable, easy to be entreated, full of mercy and good fruits, without partiality, and without hypocrisy.*" But a religion which favors the rich against the poor; which exalts the proud above the humble; which divides mankind into two classes, tyrants and slaves; which says to the man in chains, *stay there*; and to the oppressor, *oppress on*; it is a religion which may be professed and enjoyed by all the robbers and enslavers of mankind; it makes God a respecter of persons, denies his fatherhood of the race, and tramples in the dust the great truth of the brotherhood of man. All this we affirm to be true of the popular church, and the popular worship of our land and nation — a religion, a church, and a worship which, on the authority of inspired wisdom, we pronounce to be an abomination in the sight of God. In the language of Isaiah, the American church might be well addressed, "Bring no more vain ablations; incense is an abomination unto me: the new moons and Sabbaths, the calling of assemblies, I cannot away with; it is iniquity even the solemn meeting. Your new moons and your appointed feasts my soul hateth. They are a trouble to me; I am weary to bear them; and when ye spread forth your hands I will hide mine eyes from you. Yea! when ye make many prayers, I will not hear. YOUR HANDS ARE FULL OF BLOOD; cease to do evil, learn to do well; seek judgment; relieve the oppressed; judge for the fatherless; plead for the widow."

The American church is guilty, when viewed in connection with what it is doing to uphold slavery; but it is superlatively guilty when viewed in connection with its ability to abolish slavery. The sin of which it is guilty is one of omission as well as of commission. Albert Barnes but uttered what the common sense of every man at all observant of the actual state of the case will receive as truth, when he declared that "There is no power out of the church that could sustain slavery an hour, if it were not sustained in it."

Let the religious press, the pulpit, the Sunday school, the conference meeting, the great ecclesiastical, missionary, Bible and tract associations of the land array their immense powers against slavery and slaveholding; and the whole system of crime and blood would be scattered to the winds; and that they do not do this involves them in the most awful responsibility of which the mind can conceive.

In prosecuting the anti-slavery enterprise, we have been asked to spare the church, to spare the ministry; but *how*, we ask, could such a thing be done? We are met on the threshold of our efforts for the redemption of the slave, by the church and ministry of the country, in battle arrayed against us; and we are compelled to fight or flee. From *what* quarter, I beg to know, has proceeded a fire so deadly upon our ranks, during the last two years, as from the Northern pulpit? As the champions of oppressors, the chosen men of American theology have appeared — men, honored for their so-called piety, and their real learning. The Lords of Buffalo, the Springs of New York, the Lathrops of Auburn, the Coxes and Spencers of Brooklyn, the Gannets and Sharps of Boston, the Deweys of Washington, and other great religious lights of the land have, in utter denial of the authority of *Him* by whom they professed to be called to the ministry, deliberately taught us, against the example or the Hebrews and against the remonstrance of the Apostles, they teach *that we ought to obey man's law before the law of God.*

My spirit wearies of such blasphemy; and how such men can be supported, as the "standing types and representatives of Jesus Christ," is a mystery which I leave others to penetrate. In speaking of the American church, however, let it be distinctly understood that I mean the great mass of the religious organizations of our land. There are exceptions, and I thank God that there are. Noble men may be found, scattered all over these Northern States, of whom Henry Ward Beecher of Brooklyn, Samuel J. May of Syracuse, and my esteemed friend (Rev. R. R. Raymond) on the platform, are shining examples; and let me say further, that upon these men lies the duty to inspire our ranks with high religious faith and zeal, and to cheer us on in the great mission of the slave's redemption from his chains.

One is struck with the difference between the attitude of the American church towards the antislavery movement, and that occupied by the churches in England towards a similar movement in that country. There, the church, true to its mission of ameliorating, elevating, and improving the condition of mankind, came forward promptly, bound up the wounds of the West Indian slave, and restored him to his liberty. There, the question of emancipation was a high religious question. It was demanded, in the name of humanity, and according to the law of the living God. The Sharps, the Clarksons, the Wilberforces, the Buxtons, and Burchells and the Knibbs, were alike famous for their piety, and for their philanthropy. The anti-slavery movement *there* was not an anti-church movement, for the reason that the church took its full share in prosecuting that movement: and the anti-slavery movement in this country will cease to be an anti-church movement, when the church of this country shall assume a favorable, instead of a hostile position towards that movement. Americans! your republican politics, not less than your republican religion, are flagrantly inconsistent. You boast of your love of liberty, your superior civilization, and your pure Christianity, while the whole political power of the nation (as embodied in the two great political parties), is solemnly pledged to support and perpetuate the enslavement of three millions of your countrymen. You hurl your anathemas at the crowned headed tyrants of Russia and Austria, and pride yourselves on your Democratic institutions, while you yourselves consent to be the mere *tools* and *bodyguards* of the tyrants of Virginia and Carolina. You invite to your shores fugitives of oppression from abroad, honor them with banquets, greet them with ovations, cheer them, toast them, salute them, protect them, and pour out your money to them like water; but the fugitives from your own land you advertise, hunt, arrest, shoot and kill. You glory in your refinement and your universal education yet you maintain a system as barbarous and dreadful as ever stained the character of a nation — a system begun in avarice, supported in pride, and perpetuated in cruelty. You shed tears over fallen Hungary, and make the sad story of her wrongs the theme of your poets, statesmen and orators, till your gallant sons are ready to fly to arms to vindicate her cause against her oppressors; but, in regard to the ten thousand wrongs of the American slave, you would enforce the strictest silence, and would hail him as an enemy of the nation who dares to make those wrongs the subject of public discourse! You are all on fire at the mention of liberty for France or for Ireland; but are as cold as an iceberg at the thought of liberty for the enslaved of America.

You discourse eloquently on the dignity of labor; yet, you sustain a system which, in its very essence, casts a stigma upon labor. You can bare your bosom to the storm of British artillery to throw off a three penny tax on tea; and yet wring the last hard-earned farthing from the grasp of the black laborers of your country. You profess to believe "that, of one blood, God made all nations of men to dwell on the face of all the earth," and hath commanded all men, everywhere to love one another; yet you notoriously hate, (and glory in your hatred), all men whose skins are not colored like your own. You declare, before the world, and are understood by the world to declare, that you "*hold these truths to be self evident, that all men are created equal; and are endowed by their Creator with certain inalienable rights; and that, among these are, life, liberty, and the pursuit of happiness*;" and yet, you hold securely, in a bondage which, according to your own Thomas Jefferson, "*is worse than ages of that which your fathers rose in rebellion to oppose*," a *seventh part* of the inhabitants of your country.

Fellow-citizens! I will not enlarge further on your national inconsistencies. The existence of slavery in this country brands your republicanism as a sham, your humanity as a base pretence, and your Christianity as a lie. It destroys your moral power abroad; it corrupts your politicians at home. It saps the foundation of religion; it makes your name a hissing, and a bye-word to a mocking earth. It is the antagonistic force in your government, the only thing that seriously disturbs and endangers your *Union*. It fetters your progress; it is the enemy of improvement, the deadly foe of education; it fosters pride; it breeds insolence; it promotes vice; it shelters crime; it is a curse to the earth that supports it; and yet, you cling to it, as if it were the sheet anchor of all your hopes. Oh! be warned! be warned! a horrible reptile is coiled up in your nation's bosom; the venomous creature is nursing at the tender breast of your youthful republic; *for the love of God*, tear away, and fling from you the hideous monster, and *let the weight of twenty millions crush and destroy it forever*!

But it is answered in reply to all this, that precisely what I have now denounced is, in fact, guaranteed and sanctioned by the Constitution of the United States; that the right to hold and to hunt slaves is a part of that Constitution framed by the illustrious Fathers of this Republic.

Then, I dare to affirm, notwithstanding all I have said before, your fathers stooped, basely stooped

> *To palter with us in a double sense:*
> *And keep the word of promise to the ear,*
> *But break it to the heart.*

And instead of being the honest men I have before declared them to be, they were the verist imposters that ever practiced on mankind. This is the inevitable conclusion, and from it there is no escape. But I differ from those who charge this baseness on the framers of the Constitution of the United States. It is a slander upon their memory, at least, so I believe. There is not time now to argue the constitutional question at length — nor have I the ability to discuss it as it ought to be discussed. The subject has been handled with masterly power by Lysander Spooner, Esq., by

William Goodell, by Samuel E. Sewall, Esq., and last, though not least, by Gerritt Smith, Esq. These gentlemen have, as I think, fully and clearly vindicated the Constitution from any design to support slavery for an hour.

Fellow-citizens! there is no matter in respect to which, the people of the North have allowed themselves to be so ruinously imposed upon, as that of the pro-slavery character of the Constitution. In that instrument I hold there is neither warrant, license, nor sanction of the hateful thing; but, interpreted as it ought to be interpreted, the Constitution is a GLORIOUS LIBERTY DOCUMENT. Read its preamble, consider its purposes. Is slavery among them? Is it at the gateway? or is it in the temple? It is neither. While I do not intend to argue this question on the present occasion, let me ask, if it be not somewhat singular that, if the Constitution were intended to be, by its framers and adopters, a slave-holding instrument, why neither slavery, slaveholding, nor slave can anywhere be found in it. What would be thought of an instrument, drawn up, legally drawn up, for the purpose of entitling the city of Rochester to a track of land, in which no mention of land was made? Now, there are certain rules of interpretation, for the proper understanding of all legal instruments. These rules are well established. They are plain, common-sense rules, such as you and I, and all of us, can understand and apply, without having passed years in the study of law. I scout the idea that the question of the constitutionality or unconstitutionality of slavery is not a question for the people. I hold that every American citizen has a right to form an opinion of the constitution, and to propagate that opinion, and to use all honorable means to make his opinion the prevailing one. Without this right, the liberty of an American citizen would be as insecure as that of a Frenchman. Ex-Vice-President Dallas tells us that the Constitution is an object to which no American mind can be too attentive, and no American heart too devoted. He further says, the Constitution, in its words, is plain and intelligible, and is meant for the home-bred, unsophisticated understandings of our fellow-citizens. Senator Berrien tell us that the Constitution is the fundamental law, that which controls all others. The charter of our liberties, which every citizen has a personal interest in understanding thoroughly. The testimony of Senator Breese, Lewis Cass, and many others that might be named, who are everywhere esteemed as sound lawyers, so regard the constitution. I take it, therefore, that it is not presumption in a private citizen to form an opinion of that instrument.

Now, take the Constitution according to its plain reading, and I defy the presentation of a single proslavery clause in it. On the other hand it will be found to contain principles and purposes, entirely hostile to the existence of slavery.

I have detained my audience entirely too long already. At some future period I will gladly avail myself of an opportunity to give this subject a full and fair discussion.

Allow me to say, in conclusion, notwithstanding the dark picture I have this day presented of the state of the nation, I do not despair of this country. There are forces in operation, which must inevitably work the downfall of slavery. "The arm of the Lord is not shortened," and the doom of slavery is certain. I, therefore, leave off where I began, with hope. While drawing encouragement from the Declaration of Independence, the great principles it contains, and the genius of American Institutions, my spirit is also cheered by the obvious tendencies of the age. Nations do not now stand in the same relation to each other that they did ages ago. No nation can now shut itself up from the surrounding world, and trot round in the same old path of its fathers without interference. The time was when such could be done. Long established customs of hurtful character could formerly fence themselves in, and do their evil work with social impunity. Knowledge was then confined and enjoyed by the privileged few, and the multitude walked on in mental darkness. But a change has now come over the affairs of mankind. Walled cities and empires have become unfashionable. The arm of commerce has borne away the gates of the strong city. Intelligence is penetrating the darkest corners of the globe. It makes its pathway over and under the sea, as well as on the earth. Wind, steam, and lightning are its chartered agents. Oceans no longer divide, but link nations together. From Boston to London is now a holiday excursion. Space is comparatively annihilated. Thoughts expressed on one side of the Atlantic, are distinctly heard on the other. The far off and almost fabulous Pacific rolls in grandeur at our feet. The Celestial Empire, the mystery of ages, is being solved. The fiat of the Almighty, "Let there be Light," has not yet spent its force. No abuse, no outrage whether in taste, sport or avarice, can now hide itself from the all-pervading light. The iron shoe, and crippled foot of China must be seen, in contrast with nature. Africa must rise and put on her yet unwoven garment. "Ethiopia shall stretch out her hand unto God." In the fervent aspirations of William Lloyd Garrison, I say, and let every heart join in saying it:

> *God speed the year of jubilee*
> *The wide world o'er*
> *When from their galling chains set free,*
> *Th' oppress'd shall vilely bend the knee,*
> *And wear the yoke of tyranny*
> *Like brutes no more.*
> *That year will come, and freedom's reign,*
> *To man his plundered fights again*
> *Restore.*
>
> *God speed the day when human blood*
> *Shall cease to flow!*
> *In every clime be understood,*
> *The claims of human brotherhood,*
> *And each return for evil, good,*
> *Not blow for blow;*
> *That day will come all feuds to end.*
> *And change into a faithful friend*
> *Each foe.*
>
> *God speed the hour, the glorious hour,*
> *When none on earth*
> *Shall exercise a lordly power,*
> *Nor in a tyrant's presence cower;*
> *But all to manhood's stature tower,*
> *By equal birth!*
> *That hour will come, to each, to all,*
> *And from his prison-house, the thrall*
> *Go forth.*

Until that year, day, hour, arrive,
With head, and heart, and hand I'll strive,
To break the rod, and rend the gyve,
The spoiler of his prey deprive —
So witness Heaven!
And never from my chosen post,
Whate'er the peril or the cost,
Be driven.

BIBLIOGRAPHY

Allen, Theodore W. *The Invention of the White Race: Racial Oppression and Social Control*, New Expanded Edition, VersoBooks (2012)

Althusser, Louis. *Politic and History: Montesquieu, Rousseau, Marx, Ben Brewster* (trans.) London, VersoBooks (2007)

Anderson, Fred and Andrew Cayton. *The Dominion of War: Empire and Liberty in North America, 1500 – 2000*, New York: Viking Penguin (2005)

Armitage, David. *The Declaration of Independence: A Global History*, Cambridge, Massachusetts: Harvard University Press (2007)

Ashcraft, Richard. *Revolutionary Politics and Locke's Two Treaties of Government*, Princeton University Press, Princeton (1988)

Auden, W. H. and Louis Kronenberger. *The Viking Book of Aphorisms*, New York: Viking Press (1966)

Banks, Taunya Lovell. *Dangerous Women: Elizabeth Key's Freedom Suit – Subjecthood and Racialized Identity in Seventeen Century Colonial Virginia*, Digital Commons Law, University of Maryland Law School (April 2009)

Barro, Robert J. *Determinants of Economic Growth: A Cross Country Empirical Study* (Cambridge, Massachusetts, MIT Press (1997)

Bell, Derrick. *Race, Racism and American Law*. Boston, M.A. Little, Brown & Co. Law Book Division (1992)

Bennett, Lerone, Jr. *The Shaping of Black America*, New York: Penguin (1993)

Bennet, Lerone, Jr. *Before the Mayflower: A History of the American Negro in America 1619-1964*. Chicago, Il. Johnson Publishing Co. (1966)

Berlin, Ira. *Many Thousands Gone: The First Two Centuries of Slavery in North America*, Cambridge, Mass.: Harvard University Press (1998)

Blackburn, Robin. *The Making of New World Slavery: From the Baroque to the Modern 1492-1800*, London, New York: Versobooks (1997)

Blight, David W. *A Slave No More: Two Men Who Escaped to Freedom, Including Their Own Narratives of Emancipation*, Boston, Mass.: Houghton Mifflin, (2007)

Blumrosen, Alfred W. and Ruth G. Blumrosen, *Slave Nation: How Slavery United the Colonies & Sparked the American Revolution*, Naperville, Illinois: Sourcebooks, Inc. (2005)

Bogus, Carl T. *The Hidden History of the Second Amendment*, 31 U.C. Davis Law Review (1998)

Brewster, Holly. *By Birth or Consent*, UNC Press: Chapel Hill (2007)

Bristow, Peggy. *We're Rooted Here and They Can't Pull Us Up: Essays in African Canadian Women's History*, University of Toronto Press (1994)

Brookhiser, Richard. *Founding Father: Rediscovering George Washington*, New York: Free Press (1996)

Burstein, Andrew. *America's Jubilee: How in 1826 a Generation Remembered Fifty Years of Independence*, New York: Knopf (2001)

Carpenter, A. H. *Naturalization in England and the American Colonies*, The American Historical Review, American Historical Association (1904)

Catteral, Helen Tunnicliff. *Judicial Cases Concerning American Slavery and the Negro, Vol. I: Cases from he Courts of England, Virginia, West Virginia, and Kentucky, Washington, D.C.*: Carnegie Institution of Washington (1926)

Christian, Charles M. *Black Saga: The African American Experience: A Chronology*, Washington, D.C.: Civitas (1999)

Churchill, Ward. *Fantasies of the Master Race*, Monroe, ME: Common Courage Press (1992)

Davis, David Brion. *Inhuman Bondage: The Rise and Fall of Slavery in the New World*, New York: Oxford University Press (2006)

Davis, Kenneth C. *A Nation Rising: Untold Tales of Flawed Founders, Fallen Heroes, and Forgotten Fighters from America's Hidden History*, HarperCollins Publishers (2010)

Day, Thomas. Fragment of an original letter on the Slavery of the Negroes, written the year 1776, London: Printed for John Stockdale (1784), Boston Re-printed by Garrison & Knapp, at the office of *"The Liberator"* (1831), p. 10 Retrieved 2014-02-26: "If there be an object truly ridiculous in nature, it is an American patriot, signing resolutions of independency with one hand, and with the other brandishing a whip over his affrighted slaves."

de Bracton, Henry. *Of the Laws and Customs of England*, 2 tans. Samuel E. Thorne, Cambridge, MA: Harvard University Press, Belknap Press (1968)

Doe, Norman. *Fundamental Authority in Late Medieval English Law*, Cambridge: Cambridge University Press (1990)

Douglass, Frederick. *Autobiographies (Narratives of the Life of Frederick Douglass, an American Slave; My Bondage and My Freedom; Life and Times of Frederick Douglass)*, New York: Library of America (1994)

Ellis, Joseph J. *American Sphinx: The Character of Thomas Jefferson*, New York: Knopf (1997)

Finkelman, Paul. *Emancipation and Reconstruction: Vol. 3. Race, Law and American History 1700-1990.* New York, N.Y. Garland Pub. (1992)

Fitzpatrick, John C. Editor. *The Writings of George Washington from the Original Manuscript Sources 1745-1799, Vol. 26, 1January 1783 – 10 June 1783.* Washington D. C.: United States Government Printing Office

Fogel, Robert and Stanley Engerman, *Time on the Cross: The Economics of American Negro Slavery*, New York: W.W. Norton and Company (1974)

Forner, Eric. *Give me Liberty: An American History*, Volume I, New York: W. W. Norton & Co. (2006)

Franklin, John Hope and Alfred A. Moss, Jr. *From Slavery to Freedom: A History of African Americans*, 8th ed. New York: Knopf (2009)

Genovese, Eugene D. *Roll Jordan, Roll: The World the Slaves Made*, New York: Random House (1974)

Gordon-Reed, Annette. *Thomas Jefferson and Sally Hemings: An American Controversy*, Charlottesville: University Press of Virginia (1997)

Hadden, Sally E. *Slave Patrols: Law and Violence in Virginia and the Carolinas*, Harvard University Press (2003)

Hayek, Friedrich. Law. *Legislation and Liberty*, Volume 3: The Political Order of a Free People (1973)

Hayek, Friedrich. *The Constitution of Liberty* (Definitive ed.), Chicago: University of Chicago Press, ISBN 978-0-226-31539-3 (2011)

Hayek, Friedrich. *The Road to Serfdom,* Chicago: University of Chicago Press (1994)

Historical Demographics, Economic and Social Data: The United States 1790-1970: Historical Statistics of the United States, ICPSR Study

Hoffman, Ronald and Peter J. Albert. *Peace and the Peacemakers: The Treaty of 1783*, University of Virginia Press (1981)

Hoyt, Edward A. *Naturalization Under the American Colonies: Signs of a New Community*, Political Science Quarterly, Academy of Political Science (1952)

Ignatief, Michael. *American Exceptionalism and Human Rights*, Princeton University Press (2005)

Isenbberg, Nancy. *Fallen Founder: The Life of Aaron Burr*, New York: Viking (2007)

Johansen, Robert Walter. *Manifest Destiny and Empire: American Antebellum Expansionism*, Texas A & M (1997) Journals of the Continental Congress, Library of Congress

Kaplan, Sidney. *The Domestic Insurrections of the Declaration of Independence*, Journal of Negro History (PDF) Vol, 61, No. 3 (July 1976)

Kidd, Thomas. God of Liberty: *A Religious History of the American Revolution*, New York: Basic Books (2010)

Ketcham, Ralph. *James Madison: A Biography*, Macmillan (1971)

Kettner, James H. *The Development of American Citizenship, 1608-1870*, University of North Carolina Press (1978)

Koh, Harold. *American Exceptionalism and Human Rights*, Princeton University Press, (2005)

Kolchin, Peter. *American Slavery: 1619 to 1877*, New York: Hill and Wang (1994)

Kulikoff, Allan. *Tobacco and Slaves: The Development of Southern Cultures in the Chesapeake, 1680 – 1800*, Chapel Hill and London: University of North Carolina Press (1986)

Lepore, Jill. *New York Burning: Liberty, Slavery and Conspiracy in Eighteenth Century Manhattan*, New York: Knopf (2005)

Levy, Leonard W. and Kenneth L. Karst. *Encyclopedia of the American Constitution*, Macmillan (1987)

Locke, John. *Second Treatise of Government*, ed. C. B. Macpherson, Hackett Publishing Co., Inc. (1980)

Lovejoy, Paul E. *Transformation of Slavery: A History of Slavery in Africa*, London Cambridge University Press (2012)

Maier, Pauline. *American Scripture: Making the Declaration of Independence*, New York: Knopf (1997)

Main, Jackson Turner. *The Social Structure of Revolutionary America*, Princeton, N. J.: Princeton University Press (1965)

McPherson, James. *Abraham Lincoln and the Second American Revolution*, New York: Oxford University Press (1991)

Meltzer, Milton. *Slavery: A World History*, Da Capo Press: New York (1971)

Middlekauff, Robert. *Glorious Cause: The American Revolution, 1763-1789*, Oxford University Press (2005)

Miller, John C. *Crisis in Freedom: The Alien and Sedition Acts*, New York: Little, Brown and Company (1951)

Morgan, Edmund S. *American Slavery, American Freedom: The Ordeal of Colonial Virginia*, W.W. Norton & Company, Inc. New York (1975)

Namier, Lewis B. *King George III: A Study in Personality; in Personality and Power*, London: Hamish Hamilton (1955)

Nash, Gary B. *The Unknown American Revolution: The Unruly Birth of Democracy and the Struggle to Create America*, Penguin Random House (2006)

Paine, Thomas. (January 14, 1776). *Common Sense: Paine Collected Writings*, The Library of America, ISBN 978-1-4286-2200-5

Pangle, Thomas. *Montesquieu's Philosophy of Liberalism: A Commentary on The Spirit of the Laws*, Chicago: University of Chicago Press (1973)

Pease, Donald E. *The New American Exceptionalism*, University of Minnesota Press, (2009)

Presser, Stephen B. *Book Review*, 14 Const. Comment., 229 (1997)

Poser, Norman. *Lord Mansfield, Justice in the Age of Reason*, (McGill-Queen's University Press, Canada (2013)

Quarles, Benjamin. *The Negro in the Making of America*, New York: Macmillan (1987)

Rahe, Paul. *Montesquieu and the Logic of Liberty*, New Haven: Yale University Press (2009)

Rediker, Marcus. *The Slave Ship: A Human History*, New York: Viking (2007)

Reid, John Phillip. *Constitutional History of the American Revolution: The Authority of Rights*, University of Wisconsin Press (1986)

Reinstein, Robert J. *Completing the Constitution: The Declaration of Independence, Bill of Rights and Fourteenth Amendment*, 66 Temple L. Rev. 361, 362-363 (1993)

Risch, Erna. *Encouragement of Immigration: As Revealed in Colonial Legislation*, The Virginia Magazine of History and Biography, Virginia Historical Society (1937)

Russell, Conrad. *The Origins of the English Civil War*, Macmillian, ISBN 0333124006 (1973)

Rutherfurd, Edward. *London: The Novel*, The Ballantine Publishing Group (1997)

Shientaig, Bernard L. *Lord Mansfield Revisited: A Modern Assessment*, 10 Fordham L. Rev. 345 (1941)

Smith, Thomas W. *The Slave in Canada"* Collections of the Nova Scotia Historical Society, X (1896-98)

Stampp, Kenneth M. *The Peculiar Institution: Slavery in the Ante-Bellum South*, New York: Vintage (1984)

Stannard, David E. *American Holocaust: The Conquest of the New World*, New York: Oxford University Press (1992)

Stein, Peter. *The Classical and Influence of the Roman Civil Law: Historical Essays*, London: The Hambledon Press (1988)

Szatmary, David P. *Shay's Rebellion: The Making of an Agrarian Insurrection*, University of Massachusetts Press (1980)

Tocqueville, Alexis de. *Democracy in America*, Trans. George Lawrence, New York: Perennial (1988)

Toppin, Edgar A. *A Biographical History of Blacks in America since 1528*, New York: David McKay Company, Inc. (1971)

Trevelyan, George O. *George III and Charles Fox: The Concluding Part of the American Revolution*, Longmans, Green (1912)

Wiecek, William M. *Somerset: Lord Mansfield and the Legitimacy of Slavery in the Anglo-American World*, University of Chicago Law Review, Vol. 42, No. 1 (Autumn 1976)

Williams, Eric. *Capitalism & Slavery with a New Introduction* Colin A. Palmer. Chapel Hill &

London: The University of North Carolina Press (1994)

Willis, Garry. *A Necessary Evil: A History of American Distrust of Government*, Simon & Schuster, (1999)

Wilson, James Grant. *Dunmore John Murray, Appleton's' Cyclopedia of American Biography*, New York (1900)

Wilson, Theodore Brantner. *The Black Codes of the South*, University of Alabama Press (1965)

Wise, S. M. *Though the Heavens May Fall: The Landmark Trial that Led to the End of Human Slavery*, Cambridge, Mass. (2005)

Wood, Gordon S. *The Creation of the American Republic, 1776-1787*, University of North Carolina Press (1969)

Woolhouse, Roger. *Locke: A Biography*, Cambridge University Press, Cambridge (2007)

Wright, Gavin. *Slavery and American Economic Development*, Baton Rouge, Louisiana: Louisiana State University (2006)

Yaffe, Gideon. *Liberty Worth the Name: Locke on Free Agency*, Princeton University Press: Princeton (2000)

Made in the USA
Monee, IL
10 September 2021